It's One of Them!

It's One of Them!

Living with Spinal Muscular Atrophy

By Grace Saunders

authorHOUSE®

AuthorHouse™ UK
1663 Liberty Drive
Bloomington, IN 47403 USA
www.authorhouse.co.uk
Phone: 0800.197.4150

Published by AuthorHouse   11/25/2014

ISBN: 978-1-4969-9753-1 (sc)
ISBN: 978-1-4969-9752-4 (hc)
ISBN: 978-1-4969-9754-8 (e)

Library of Congress Control Number: 2014921199

Any people depicted in stock imagery provided by Thinkstock are models, and such images are being used for illustrative purposes only. Certain stock imagery © Thinkstock.

This book is printed on acid-free paper.

Because of the dynamic nature of the Internet, any web addresses or links contained in this book may have changed since publication and may no longer be valid. The views expressed in this work are solely those of the author and do not necessarily reflect the views of the publisher, and the publisher hereby disclaims any responsibility for them.

CONTENTS

About the Author ix

Prologue xi

Chapter One   Where Life Begins 1

Chapter Two   In This Life 9

Chapter Three   Live To Tell 17

Chapter Four   This Used To Be My Playground 25

Chapter Five   Who's That Girl 39

Chapter Six   I'm So Stupid 49

Chapter Seven   Rescue Me 57

Chapter Eight   Little Star 65

Chapter Nine   The Beast Within 79

Chapter Ten   Causing a Commotion 87

Chapter Eleven   Hello and Goodbye 99

Chapter Twelve   Girl Gone Wild 111

Chapter Thirteen   Don't Tell Me 127

Chapter Fourteen   Keep it Together 137

Chapter Fifteen   Till Death Us Do Part 149

Chapter Sixteen   Take a Bow 163

For Paul

About the Author

Sometimes in life you seem to travel full circle with people coming and going in your life. Grace is one of these people. Having met at the age of eleven years old, we had that close bond as friends throughout school and the formative teenage years. Sharing and experiencing the music and fashion of the eighties. Eventually going to the same college but somehow following different paths for the next twenty-one years.

I have always believed that people have soul mates, but you have to encounter many obstacles living life before fate brings you together. This is precisely what happened with Grace and me. Having spent so many years with no contact, we were eventually reunited, and I am proud to say have since married.

The expression "It's one of them," was something I had not heard until I moved to Coventry. I hear it a lot from people I work with, and I have to say Grace uses it a lot. But it is so fitting to Grace's attitude toward her life and past experiences.

I never hear Grace moan about what she has been through, for I think it has made her stronger and more determined to succeed in whatever she decides to do. I am very proud of my wife and know this book will inspire many people to make the most of life. Learn from your mistakes, remember to have a wicked sense of humor, and love the people who treat you well.

James Saunders

PROLOGUE

I turn 45 next year and that's quite an achievement for somebody like me. People moan about turning 40, I didn't complain once, I embraced it! I'm an ordinary middle aged woman, a Mum and a wife; I have a nice home, pets and a car. I've written this book for a few reasons; the first reason is it's been great therapy, probably better than any counselling. Secondly, I have a story to tell and hopefully it will help others whether they have children with my disability, or if they suffer from the same condition as me, or whether they've been through the traumas I've been through, but I think there's something here for a lot of people. Thirdly, this is my side of the story, there are two sides to every story but I wanted people to know mine and more importantly the truth. Everybody has skeletons in their closet and I've gone through my fair share of problems and heartache. I'm still here to tell my tales, my tragedies, and my happy days (and hopefully still lots to come); I'm still sane and smiling!

So what can I tell you about me? I like to laugh; I have a very sarcastic sense of humour. I try not to take life too seriously; I've learnt to let things go over my head more, I've learnt not to complain too much about things because there is always someone worse off than you. I can't be doing with people who moan about the slightest little things and don't even get me started on the youngsters of today who really haven't got a clue. I have never felt sorry for myself, I've always said that I wouldn't be me if I didn't have this disability, this is me.

"I never hear you complain Grace" people say. But every day is a struggle and that's the life I was dealt, so I've made the most of it.

I love my music. Music is something I could do growing up; I would always be sat in my bedroom singing into a microphone that wasn't even plugged in and usually to Abba. I wanted to be Agnetha 'the blonde one' or failing that Olivia Newton John. I loved musicals and still do. Fame, Grease, Xanadu were all huge when I was a child and when The Kids of Fame came out I was in my element, I loved it!

I love anything camp, big glitter balls, Kylie Minogue, Eurovision and disco. I've always joked that when my time is up I want half naked gay men carrying my coffin and going out to Kylie's 'Your Disco Needs You'.

I don't take a lot of crap, if somebody hurts or says anything bad about me or my family then our relationship is over. I always gave people second chances but not any more, if your so called friends can shit on you, then they don't deserve second chances. In the past I've given people all of me but I've hardened up because I've had to. I'm genuine, if you want my advice I will give it to you, if you don't want to hear what I have to say then don't ask me. If a friend asks my opinion on her dress, if I don't like it I will tell her, I try to be honest but without upsetting anyone either. I am also very soft and hate confrontation but when something really needs to be said I will say it.

I love my own space and my own company but I also love company too. I love socialising and will talk to anyone, especially after a bottle of wine. I can be the party animal or I can be the quiet one in the corner, depending on my mood and my energy.

I'm a huge Madonna fan and that's the reason I thought I would use her song titles as chapters. I've followed her from the beginning and have seen her in concert a few times and hopefully one day I will see her again.

I'm a massive Marilyn Monroe fan and she's been part of my life since I discovered her at 15, I read a book about her and was hooked. People always ask me what it is about her that I love. Marilyn was extremely beautiful, a natural beauty unlike today's celebrities, yes she had a little bit of work done but there was nothing like Botox around then and she was on the larger side, a real woman. She was also very misunderstood, not the dumb blonde everybody thought she was. She was a very lonely person, used and abused by many and I would love to have been her friend and been there for her. I feel some connection with her, I have no idea why.

I have to tell you one weird experience with her. I had a shelf in my bedroom with all her books on and on the anniversary of her death, some years ago the screw for the shelf decided to loosen and all the books fell off, landing on my computer and the floor. The shelf had been up for six years without a problem but the time was 6am in the morning and working it out, that would have been 10pm Los Angeles time, which is where Marilyn both lived and died and is the time they believe she would have passed away. I woke thinking it was an earth quake or something, I was facing the opposite wall and when my Mum came in to see what was going on she said. "Your shelf with your Marilyn books has broken". When I told her what day it was she too said it was weird. So Marilyn, if that was you giving me a sign, I heard you!

I'm a very spiritual person too. I've been told I have some kind of gift by other psychics but that I just don't know how to use it properly. I can read Tarot Cards but I can't do it without looking through a book, once I have read the meaning of the cards I can kind of pick up on what it's trying to say for that person. I did a reading for a friend once and his sister-in-law was pregnant with twins. Well I told him that two boys would be born in the summer but right up until they were born she was told it was a boy and a girl. "No, it's definitely two boys". I kept saying. I got a phone call from my friend to say the babies had been born and what were they? Yes, two boys!

My dreams are also very vivid too, always mixed up, in colour and I believe that's how I get some of my messages. For example, I dreamt years ago that Madonna had died and she was on the front pages of all the papers. Two days later Madonna was on the front pages for falling off a horse and breaking some bones. I also get a really weird, sickly feeling when something serious is about to happen. For instance, when my daughter's Granddad was rushed into hospital and then, on the day he sadly died I felt strange and couldn't explain it. I have that feeling when something is going to happen but I really don't know what it is. I also had it a couple of days before my daughters Nana, who had cancer, collapsed and was taken to hospital. I hate getting that feeling now. I definitely have something, I always say that my mind's open a bit more to things like that because it's making up for my weak body.

I'm into Astrology; I'm a Pisces and a typical one. A dreamer, constantly living in a fantasy land, imaginative, sensitive, feeling, spiritual, soul growth, suffering, artistic, overly emotional, romantic and poetic, very caring, compassionate and reflective. Every one of those is me. Whenever I meet someone I always ask what star sign they are so that I can get a bit more of an idea about them and definitely in my dating days.

I hope that gives you an idea of the sort of person I am, nothing complex, very down to earth, what you see is what you get, probably too opinionated sometimes but that's just me, but physical appearance is a whole different story!

CHAPTER ONE

Where Life Begins

I was born in the spring of 1970. Lee Marvin's 'Wanderin Star' was number one in the charts, the Beatles were about to split. The Vietnam War was going on, Edward Heath became Prime Minister and Jimi Hendrix died.

I was born on the 14ᵗʰ March, 6lb 12ounces, a perfectly healthy baby girl. My parents were working class, my Dad, was an Agricultural Contractor and my Mum, worked for the council. My Dad's roots are half Yorkshire and half Cockney, his Mum, my Nan, was born 'within the sound of the Bow Bells' which traditionally means you were a real Cockney. My Granddad was from up north in Yorkshire, they met after the First World War, when he was a butler and my Nan a maid in Hatfield, Hertfordshire, yes very Downton Abbey! My Dad was the second eldest of four boys. He was the cheekiest of the boys; my Mum always said "Your Father may not have been the best looking one but he was the one with the nicest personality".

My Mum was an only child and lived in Essendon, sadly her father died in 1973, he had Reynaud's Disease which is a condition that causes discolouration to your fingers and toes and other area's of your body. I just about remember my Granddad; all I remember was him having funny fingers. He had strokes because his arteries were blocked and died of Arterial Sclerosis. Funnily enough my Mums current husband has Reynauds; she says jokingly that it must be following her. Her mother wasn't a typical Nan to my brother and I, she loved her bingo and smoked, she always got the bus over to us on a Tuesday, every Tuesday without fail, until she died in 1989 after her battle with cancer.

My Mum and Dad met when she was 15 and my Dad 19, today the age gap would be talked about and would be a huge problem because my Mum was underage, but back then nobody batted an eye lid. They married four years later and lived in Hatfield. My Mum's cousin also married my Dads Brother so her cousin is also her sister-in-law and this would be bought up later in life because of my brother and me having the same condition.

I was born at the QEII hospital in Welwyn Garden City. My Dad went to the football that afternoon, which has always been a running joke, football was more important than his new baby daughter. Dad always said when I got married not to have it on a Saturday when his football team was playing at home, I got married on a Friday so no matches that day!

For months I was healthy, a very sickly baby, but I was perfectly normal. Mum said she would put me in a nice pretty dress and straight away I would throw up. But I didn't seem as strong as normal infants, floppier, I couldn't do things like sit up without help or start walking, Mum and Dad just thought I was a lazy baby. But as time went on they realised something wasn't right with me, I wasn't progressing like a normal baby.

After tests and a muscle biopsy they diagnosed a condition called Spinal Muscular Atrophy. SMA is a genetic neuromuscular condition causing weakness to the muscles. My Mum and Dad both had the same defected gene, if my Mum had conceived a baby with another man the baby would have been fine, unless the man also had the defected gene. The same goes for my Dad with another woman. Parents with the gene have a 1 in 4 chance of having a baby with SMA. I've found out recently that it's also called 'Floppy Baby Syndrome'. SMA affects about 1 in every 10,000 children.

There are different types of SMA and I had SMA II-III Intermediate which is in the middle. Type I (Werdnig-Hoffman disease) is the most severe. It may begin before birth or shortly afterwards (mothers may notice decreased movement of the foetus late in pregnancy), and affected babies are rarely able to lift their head or develop normal movement. Swallowing, feeding and breathing may be difficult and the child rarely survives to 2 years of age. Type II (Intermediate) usually appears within the first couple of years. The child may reach adulthood, although they may need help to sit or stand and strain on the muscles can cause complications. Type III (Kugelberg-Welander disease) is relatively mild and may be diagnosed as late as adolescence. Those affected may have problems walking or getting up from sitting.

The primary feature with SMA is the muscle weakness. SMA affects the nerves in an area of the spinal cord called the anterior horn. The nerve cells become damaged, breaking the link between the brain and the muscles. As a result, the muscles can't be used and waste away. This can lead to problems with breathing as well as motor activities such as crawling, walking, feeding and head control.

There are still no cures for SMA but you can now be screened to see if you are a carrier. Once the abnormal gene has been identified, carriers can be detected by a blood test, and antenatal screening using CVS (Chorionic Villus Sampling) is available.

I was going to need constant physiotherapy and a lot of medical care, frequent visits to the hospital for check ups, calliper fittings, splints made, calliper shoes made and operations,

I could stand at an early age with my Mum assisting me and I could crawl but that was about it, I even remember trying to sit myself up. I would be on my side and I would put the back of my hand under my chin and push myself up, you just found a way of doing things. Everybody with a disability finds a way of doing things depending on their mobility. I've weakened over the years but I will do things like type, feed myself, and do my make up etc for as long as I'm physically able, although I am finding it more difficult.

Two years after I was born my brother Ben came into the world, born at home whilst I ate liver and bacon; the liver and bacon is all I remember about that day. There was a big chance that Ben would have SMA too. The doctors did tests on him at an early age because of me and yes he also had the condition. My Mum and Dad would have to bring up 2 children with a severe disability. There wasn't the support back then like now, the odd social worker that really didn't have a clue. One social worker even said to my Mum "well at least you have two, they can keep each other company!" much to my Mums disgust!

You see I had most of the tests before my brother came along, so he didn't have to go through what I went through. I was first admitted to Westminster Children's Hospital when I was just 19 months old for a Myelogram, a Lumber Puncture and various X Rays. All these tests were negative and nowhere nearer finding out what was wrong with me and the only thing I got from that particular hospital stay was Chicken Pox!

My Mum kept a record of my operations, physiotherapy etc and wow, reading back, I went through a lot. I was quite a healthy child and even as an adult I'm relatively healthy. I had tonsillitis a lot and ended up having my tonsils removed when I was 4. I just about remember this; I remember eating the ice cream after the operation because that was the only thing you were allowed to eat.

I had my Muscle Biopsy when I was 2, which consisted of taking a piece of muscle out of the bottom of my leg; the scar is still quite prominent now. They found out that the nerves in my spine were 'paralysed'.

I had to go to the Q.E.II hospital in Welwyn Garden City twice a week for physiotherapy; we were living in Hatfield at the time so it was quite a lot of trips backwards and forwards.

In the June of 1972 I was fitted with my first set of callipers, how cute must those callipers have looked? I was only little. I was having new callipers until I stopped walking when I was 9. I'd outgrow them and so I would have to have a new set of callipers all the time.

Going in and out of hospital was normal for me, I used to hate it, but it had to be done and to be honest I didn't know any different. I didn't want to be pulled about and have physio but I knew it was to help me. My legs would be straightened, my knees pushed down, made to walk in my callipers and sometimes it was just too tiring for me. My legs and ankles would get hurt quite a lot if they were caught wrong or straightened too much. I mean, I had a green stick fracture of the femur when I was 3. There was another time when I sprained my ankles from being pushed through long grass at Whipsnade Zoo in one of those blue and white stripy double buggies, there was always some injury. When I was about 7 I was playing in my bedroom with the girls that lived upstairs. I was sat on the edge of my bed and one of them pulled me, not knowing my balance wasn't good and I ended up on the floor with a sprained knee, at the time we thought it was broken. There was also another time when I tipped over in my wheelchair outside our flat and rushed to hospital with a suspected fractured skull but luckily it was fine. My legs were forever getting caught from being lifted onto coaches or into cars, Dad always made sure he lifted us right but accidents would happen.

Ben was always the stronger one when we were kids. He would always be crawling around the house and walking in callipers with his Rollator. As Ben was a little bit more independent than me he always attended a normal mainstream school, I guess it was easier for him as being a girl I needed a little more care and help. He didn't get hurt as much as me, although there were a couple of times, both on holiday in Great Yarmouth. One time Granddad tipped him out of his chair down a step and Dad caught his leg at the caravan.

My Uncle (Dads younger brother) and his family moved to New Zealand in 1973 to start a new life. There were talks about us moving over there but New Zealand wouldn't have given the medical support Ben and I needed, they were quite behind the UK, so Mum and Dad had to forget about that idea. Mum and Dad had great friends; they always said the friends did more than family. We were always going over to Hatfield for the day to spend time with friends or they would come to us and Mum would put on the best buffet. I remember Mum and Dad going to friends for the evening and Ben and I would be put to bed upstairs and then get woken up, wrapped in a blanket and taken home at the end of the night.

Dad would drive even though he had been drinking, but I think everyone did then, you wouldn't dare do that now, not that it's okay.

Mum and Dad were always involved in activities. There was the toy library, much the same as a library where you borrowed a book but this was borrowing a toy for a couple of weeks. Can you imagine it now, the toys wouldn't be good enough for people's kids but we were more grateful back then. I remember sitting on a float (lorry) to do with the toy library for a festival and having to wave as we passed the crowds lined along the streets. They were involved in the Muscular Dystrophy group based in Hatfield. They used to do jumble sales and collecting in town. When Ben and I were older we would sit there with the collection pot or give someone a sticker when they had donated money. Mum and Dad were always involved with something; I don't know how they had the time looking after the two of us.

I was a massive Abba fan. I had posters covering my bedroom walls, annuals, soap, perfume, and dolls and was a member of the Abba fan club. I was obsessed with them; I think every little girl was at that time. Ben loved Star Wars and I Abba. I was actually lucky enough to see them at Wembley in 1979. I was in my element and feel so blessed to have actually seen them live. I don't know what happened to my Abba collection, those dolls would be worth something now.

I don't remember our first house in Hatfield but I do remember the second, a normal three bedroom council house and we lived there until it was too hard for Mum and Dad to lift us up and down the stairs. Brand new accessible flats were being built in Welwyn Garden City, which we moved to in 1976, this was my home until I left and moved to Coventry. I say accessible but all it had was low light switches and sliding doors on all the rooms, apart from Ben's bedroom. The flat was long with all the rooms going off of the main corridor. A wheel in shower that had to have tiles around it to keep the water in, not like the 'wet rooms' we have now, and a bath which they changed to a corner bath once Ben and I had left home. The living room was of average size and we had a large corner sofa in it. Directly opposite was an open space for a dining table and we could still watch TV whilst eating our dinner. My bedroom wasn't that big, the smallest of the three but I had it because it was opposite the bathroom. Mum and Dad had the middle bedroom and Ben had the one on the end. There would be Ben with his music on at one end of the flat and me the other end with mine on and Mum being driven mad in the middle. The only problem with the flat was that we had no garden. All we had was a small square bit of patio outside the living room, but it over looked a road so it wasn't private, or there was the bit in front of the flat outside the garage, but again it wasn't private. Mum would sometimes have her sun bed out there but I never bothered. I appreciate my garden so much now, it's very private and I'm always out there in the summer!

I was 6 when we moved into the flat in Welwyn. I remember the summer of '76, the highest temperatures on record. If we got burnt in those days the calamine lotion would come out and we'd be covered in it. The following year was the Queens Silver Jubilee and the street organised a street party and fancy dress. Red, white and blue was everywhere, even school put a huge outside party on. My brother won the fancy dress at the street party. My Mum made this amazing robot outfit for him made out of lots of boxes and foil, he even had a box on his head. I was in my usual Hawaiian outfit that Mum always put me in, she had a knack of making crepe flowers, but the robot won hands down! Mum was pretty creative, always knitting and making things, she made my pink party dress that I loved wearing. Every little girl had that one pretty party dress that they wore to every party, I was gutted when it got too small for me, and the second dress wasn't nearly as nice.

Living in Welwyn wasn't always happy, especially for my Mum and Dad. The flat was in a block of six in like a T shape. Our flat was one of four together, upstairs lived a family, a husband and wife with two teenage girls who we used to play with. Dad used to carry me up the stairs and sit me on their beds or they would come down and play, this is how I fell off the bed. Next door lived a couple and the wife suffered with MS and they had two teenage boys. Another family lived above them but we never saw much of them. Our 'lovely' neighbours gave Mum and Dad no end of trouble. The two boys were a nightmare to live next door to, always causing trouble and upsetting Mum. Their Mum was oblivious to it as she was house bound and the Dad, a copper just turned a blind eye to it all. I don't really remember much as I was only about 7 but I remember being scared of going out the front to play just in case they were about. They made Ben tip over in his tricycle once, made him go over the raised flower bed and he tipped. They used to make him shout rude things through the window at their Mum, it was just constant bullying. Sadly for them, their Mum died and they had to move out, which for us was such a relief when they did.

I lived in that flat till I left home at 20 and Mum and Dad lived there until they sold it and moved up to Wellingborough in 2003 which I'll bring up later. There are lots of memories in that flat, it's where I mainly grew up. Ben and I had a good childhood, travelled and were brought up properly without being spoilt, were pretty grounded and chilled thanks to Mum and Dad's brilliant parenting.

CHAPTER TWO

In This Life

I don't know how Mum and Dad coped with the two of us. Dad always worked full time, he changed jobs when I was about 12 and started working as an HGV driver starting on days and then moving on to nights. He did this until he retired. Mum had a few jobs, just something part time to get her out of the house and to have a life outside of the family; everyone needs a break. She used to work a couple of hours a night at a factory and some nights she would work from home, she'd have lots of boxes of Airwick's to put together. She would have a production line going in the living room, grab two bits, twist them together and throw in the box. She also worked at the local doctor's surgery as a receptionist; I think she secretly loved that job as it was a way of being a little bit nosy. Funny how my husband's job involves doctors surgeries now. Mum gave the job up when they moved to Wellingborough and ended up as my carer working for me for nine years.

Mum and Dad did everything for Ben and I with not that much help from social services, that's why going to a residential school was such a help for them. Having one child with a disability is hard work but can you imagine having two? Two children that couldn't get themselves dressed, bathed or toileted. Ben and I went to playgroups in the school holidays when we lived in Hatfield to give Mum a break. We also went on holidays without Mum and Dad to give them a well deserved rest.

Every outing was a mission. Sorting the two of us out, making sure there were the right facilities wherever we went, I can't imagine how hard it was for them. We had to have big enough cars to cater for us and our wheelchairs. Once we got too big to be lifted into a car Mum and Dad bought a Transit van with a tail lift so we could sit in our wheelchairs. They bought the van themselves, that's what your Mobility money was for.

Our first holiday on our own was a week up in Sheringham, Norfolk. It must have been arranged through social services and we were not looked after properly, on trips we didn't even have seat belts on. I was so homesick. Other holidays were with the Red Cross. They used to do a week where they would use a school that was empty in the holidays, turn a couple of class rooms into dormitories and have activities for us to do every day. We were assigned to one young student nurse each and they would look after us all week. I remember one of the old nurses making a big thing of me having to have a blanket around my legs all the time. "You must put the blanket behind the legs!" she would always say and it was a running joke with everyone.

The second Red Cross holiday was much better than the first one. Probably because my friend from school went too. Ben went on more holidays than me; he was in the Cubs and then the Scouts, so he was always camping or going off with the disabled Scouts to places like Gibraltar.

In 1979 Mum and Dad took us together with a Muscular Dystrophy group to Majorca. The group was made up of families and carers to help out to give the parents a break. It was an amazing holiday with lots of amazing people and the only holiday the four of us had abroad together.

In 1985 Ben and I had the holiday of a life time. It was with a charity that took sick and disabled children to Disneyland. We couldn't believe it when Mum and Dad told us we were flying to Los Angeles! We stayed in a hotel in Santa Monica called the Hacienda. I loved LA, the atmosphere was amazing. I loved the food and everywhere you went, every bar, had this lovely smell of coffee. There was a group of about forty of us and we were looked after by qualified nurses and doctors.

There were a few lads with Muscular Dystrophy, a girl who had breathing problems and had her Mum with her. Also a girl who was 9, a lot younger than me, who I had to share a room with as we were the only girls. Ben and I had a husband and wife assigned to look after us which was handy, the four of us used to go off on our own when we were allowed.

The flight was long; I couldn't go to the toilet and had to hold it until I got to the hotel which killed me. I didn't like the fact that we had to be lifted onto buses and anywhere we went we were lifted in to A Team like vans. I didn't like the staff we had, they knew better than us all of the time, how to lift me or get me comfy which was frustrating.

Every day was structured; we did cram a lot in though. We did Disneyland which was amazing and we saw David Hasselhoff at the Universal Studios, well the top of his head as there were so many people around him, good job he's tall. We had an afternoon with cops from the California Highway Patrol or CHiPs, everyone had a go on their bike but as I couldn't they just stuck a helmet on my head.

Nutsberry Farm was another adventure park where everyone convinced me to go on the log flume. "It's a nice little ride round on the log, Grace." I was put at the front and I have never been so scared, I literally couldn't feel my hands, I swear I had a panic attack, I was shaking so much.

We had a day in Hollywood. We went along Hollywood Boulevard where all the stars are and Graumans Theatre where the handprints are, Marilyn Monroe had tiny hands and I was so excited to actually see her handprints. The nurses kept promising me that they would take me to see Marilyn's grave as we weren't that far away but sadly it never happened. I thought it was a little unfair to promise that.

Ben and I were very lucky to have had that holiday: it's my dream to go again one day. When airlines get their act together and make flying more accessible for people in wheelchair. There are so many places I want to see but now I'm older I can't transfer without the hoist. So it's either sail, which costs too much or holidays in the UK.

We had a family holiday every year, whether it was the school caravan in Norfolk or Warners Holiday Park in Hayling Island. Mum and Dad always stuck to the same place as they knew it was all accessible. I loved our caravan holidays, Nan and Granddad even came with us sometimes too. The only time you would see Nanny without her teeth in was at night and one year at the beach because the weather was so warm she even took her corset off! Even now I love staying in a caravan; the smell and cosiness of one takes me back.

One of our last holidays together was when Ben and I went to Switzerland on a big coach called a Jumbulance. It was with a charity and they took people on holidays a little bit like the American one we had in 1985, but it wasn't just children. Ben had been away with them before to Italy and this time they asked me if I wanted to go. I had just started college and so I went in the October half term. The Jumbulance was amazing. It was nearly as long as two coaches together with a bendy bit in the middle as it was too long to get round bends. It had an electronic lift and down one side normal seats and the other side were beds, so you could lie down and go to sleep if you wanted. I loved this holiday, the people were lovely and looked after us really well, there were even some other kids from school.

Switzerland was beautiful; we went up the Alps in a cable car which was a breathtaking experience. I even fell in love a little bit with one of the helpers. He was tall, dark, handsome and well spoken. We started spending more and more time together and he would always sit with me whether on the coach or eating out. I remember on one of the last nights I got pretty drunk and was very sick (nothing's changed there then!) and had to be put to bed. Head in a bowl, holding my hair out of the way and once I was in bed we kissed, yuk I had just been sick, he must have been keen!

We kept in touch after the holiday, he wrote and he came to see me at college, I loved showing him off. Once he came up to see me and I had no idea he was coming, the care staff said "There's a tall, gorgeous, young man looking for you". He even came to a Five Star concert with me, he must have liked me! We just kind of lost contact, I have looked for him on the internet but nothing. But yes, Switzerland was a brilliant holiday for lots of different reasons.

We would go to Hayling Island most years with Mum and Dad. I remember going to the kids club to give them a break. We would go to the kids hut and were looked after by Green Coats, watch cartoons and sing songs. We sang 'My Bonnie Lies over the Ocean' with all the actions every single night. When the cartoons were over the Green Coats would take us back to the main concert room for the first hour of the evening's entertainment. We entered a lot of competitions, Ben won the Bonny Baby competition and once again I was dressed up in my Hawaiian outfit for some other competition. Dad even entered wearing one of my Mum's dresses and his beard finished off the look perfectly, yes my Dad did it way before you Eurovisions Conchita Wurst!

Ben and I had a good childhood. We weren't spoilt and I think that's why I appreciate everything now. At Christmas Mum and Dad didn't go over the top, not like kids are now. People today say that they're struggling but they still manage to spoil their kids and do they appreciate it? No. We didn't both have an expensive present every Christmas or birthday, if Ben needed a stereo or if I wanted a Walkman then that would be our main present, but we both didn't have something expensive every time. A lot of kids at school seemed to get everything, but there were a lot of Muscular Dystrophy boys and so their parents brought them everything while they were still around to enjoy stuff.

Mum and Dad were strict without being over the top. We got a smack when we were naughty as kids should do, you couldn't do that these days, Social Services would be on your case. Once Ben wet himself in his callipers after just being changed and he got a slap round the legs from Dad, but he never did it again. I had a mark once around my face from Dad. I was kicking off, I wouldn't swallow some tablets which he was making me have so I bit his finger, I didn't half get a smack round my cheek, so hard it did leave a mark and I think they were only vitamins. Getting a smack never did us any harm though.

Ben and I were good kids; we would fight like any other brother and sister. Ben was always hitting me as he was the stronger one; I was always saying "Mum, Ben's hit me!" We even had a chart once that we would have to tick every night if we had been good. Ben was always doing stuff to me, once when we were getting dried after a bath on Mum and Dads bed and he poured talc into my mouth, not nice! We always stuck up for each other though and both had that really silly sense of humour. Ben passed away in 2002 which I'll talk about later in this book and I really miss him, he was my baby brother.

It got more of a struggle looking after Ben and I as we got older. Dad always lifted us but I got to heavy for him, it was easier to lift me into bed rather than get the hoist out and no way could my Mum lift me and so she had to use the hoist. In the school holidays Mum got Home Help in to help as it was too much to get the pair of us up in the mornings. Mum sorted Ben out and the Home Help lady would get me up. At first they would send different ladies in which was frustrating for me as Mum and I would have to talk them through how to get me dressed and comfortable every single time. We did finally get a lovely lady called Mary who would come in every morning and get me up who I got used to. That was how it was until I went to college and finally left home, giving Mum and Dad a well deserved rest.

I have so much appreciation for Mum and Dad. To have two children with the problems Ben and I have, well they're both amazing. Mum even relied on medication for a number of years just to help her cope. It's not until recently when my daughter, Erin had her appendix out that I began to fully appreciate what they went through. Erin only had her appendix out and I was all emotional, imagine going through several major operations for two kids. It did take a toll on their marriage, not necessarily caring for Ben and me but they drifted apart, people change. They divorced in 2007 and Mum remarried the following year. They are still good friends and both live in Wellingborough now as they moved there after Ben passed away. My Dad goes for a drink with my Mum's husband and goes round their house for his dinner on a Sunday. Dad is currently seeing my Mums neighbour and they have all been on holiday together. It's so much easier being friends than fighting; being able to spend time with both of them is so much easier. Of course I was upset when I found out that their marriage was over. It doesn't matter what age you are, it's probably harder when you're older as Mum and Dad together was all I knew and I had to get used to someone else in the equation. They are all happy now and that's all that matters.

That's basically my childhood. I see all my life as chapters and that's why I've written my book like this. I've just started on the new chapter in my life and I think it will be the last one now, and a very happy last chapter it is too.

CHAPTER THREE

Live To Tell

My first operation was, as I said before, my Muscle Biopsy the day after my 2nd birthday. I don't know if I remember this particular operation or I'm just getting confused with having my tonsils being removed. I do remember lying on a bed and being wheeled into a lift to go to surgery and feeling quite frightened. I was admitted to Westminster Children's Hospital for two weeks to have tests done on me and to have the Muscle Biopsy.

I was in and out of hospital a lot up to the age of 12 and I hated it. Mum and Dad couldn't visit every day as I was in London and they had Ben to look after too. In November 1974 I stayed in the Hammersmith Hospital in London for intense Physiotherapy. Hammersmith had the SMA clinic and Ben and I were seen every six months to make decisions on our progress. When we had our check ups there were doctors, physiotherapists, junior doctors and also a professor that specialised in SMA. There were always so many people in the room; it was something you just got used to.

I stayed in Hammersmith for two weeks and had physio every day because they were trying to build up my muscles. I hated the Physiotherapist

I had assigned to me. I know you have to be cruel to be kind but I was so scared of her, she worked me so hard. She had to sit in on our clinic appointments as she had to give feedback to the doctors and just her presence in the room used to scare me. She was always hurting me, straightening my legs too much, pulling my ankles or making me walk loads. But she was only doing her job and probably very good in what she did.

I used to cry when Mum and Dad had to leave me, I bet it broke their hearts leaving me like that. Once when I went into hospital I was fine and said to Mum and Dad "I'm ok, you can go now", that upset my Mum even more.

I used to go in on a Sunday evening in time for tea and Mum and Dad would leave me when I had settled. Hospitals aren't what they're like now, Hammersmith was drab. The main TV was at the bottom of the ward where you would go and eat your meals. The food wasn't great; I remember egg salad and ice cream in the paper wrappers and jelly. Now they have menus and lovely food, it's probably a much better experience now.

When I was in for my physio I was measured for my first set of callipers. Callipers would keep my legs straight and support me so that I could walk a little bit using a Rollator. But my first set of callipers were unsuitable and I had to be measured again. A man called Mr Florence took over and he fitted all of my future callipers and shoes. Oh the lovely shoes I had to wear with them, so flattering! I remember Mr Florence as a guy with a white beard, a little like Santa and we had to go to his calliper clinic that wasn't at the hospital but still in London. I would have to have a new set of callipers every year as I was outgrowing them so quickly.

I was 8 when I had the first operation that I can remember. I had a Hip Release, in medical terms a Rectus Femoris and an Iliotibial band. I have a scar on my right knee and one just above my groin.

After the Hip Release I gradually stopped walking. As I got older and grew, it got too hard for me to move my legs and those callipers weren't the lightest of things. I didn't even have the power in my arms to wheel a normal manual wheelchair so I have been in an electric wheelchair since I was about 6. The electric wheelchairs were a lot more basic back then and very slow. If I go full speed now it's hard to keep up with me but thirty years ago the chairs were like snails. My first powered chair had the control levers on a bar at the front between my legs, not very lady like especially when wearing a skirt. The chairs easily tipped over too, somebody could just catch the handle bars and you were over on your side, not safe at all.

They wanted to keep me walking for as long as I could so I was fitted with a contraption called a Swivel Walker. How it worked was you laid the walker on the floor and then you were lifted into it. Clamps came down on your feet, clamps across your knees, though because my knees were weak I could only have the clamp on the first setting or my legs would be pushed too straight and then a thick belt around your chest. You were stood up and on the bottom there were plates that moved you forward when you swivelled from side to side, think Metal Mickey and you might have an idea! I hated standing in that thing, we were put in them to stand for a few hours during lessons at school, I never walked far in my swivel walker though, I just didn't feel safe.

At the beginning of 1980 I had another two weeks stay in Hammersmith for more intense physiotherapy and to be fitted with a Milwaukee Brace. The brace is normally used with growing adolescents to hold a 25° to 40° advancing curve. The brace is intended to minimize the progression to an acceptable level, not to correct the curvature but maintain it, but it was so uncomfortable. It was a spinal brace with a top bit that held your neck and head to stretch your back so, very surprised I was put in one of these. I had trouble moving without being weighed down by this too!

At night I had splints to wear on my legs and hands to keep everything as straight as possible, the splints on my legs were quite comfortable and I just got used to them. At first they were made from plaster and bandaged on and then they started making them out of thick sponge. The sponge was put into an oven, taken out and moulded to the part of the body. I was out of splints by about 11 luckily, that wouldn't have looked attractive in bed in my adult years! Although it would be nice to have them now to support my hands in bed on the nights I'm uncomfortable.

I didn't have the top bit of the brace for long though as I just couldn't tolerate it. I did wear the brace all the time though; it kept my top half straight. It didn't stop the curve, it was slowly getting worse but my back was comfier with the brace on.

In March 1980 I went through the most painful experience I think I have ever been through. I had an abscess in the top of my right ear. The only thing we could put it down to is catching a bad infection from the school swimming pool but we didn't know for sure. Antibiotics didn't touch it and it got so bad that I had to have it operated on, twice. They cut the top of my ear and cleared it of all the infected yucky stuff. The first operation didn't work so they had to operate a second time and still it didn't clear. Now they would have just put me on an IV drip to get the antibiotics into my blood stream but not then.

The infection was so bad that I was put into isolation for two weeks. Anyone coming into my room had to wash their hands thoroughly and put gowns and a mask on. I didn't feel like I was that infectious, I just had a very sore ear. I was so bored; being cooped up in one room for two weeks isn't fun. I had a TV and remember watching the episode of Dallas when JR was shot. I also had my tape recorder and listened to stuff like Annabel Bush. After a lot of tests they found that I had an infection called Pseudomonas, a rare virulent bacterium unresponsive to normal antibiotics, a very stubborn nasty infection that took weeks to budge. I was having jabs three times a day in my bottom and thighs and the nurses would have to squeeze the shit out of my ear a few times a day, it was horrendous. I would literally scream the ward down as it was so painful. I was let out for the day to go to an airshow with Mum and Dad but they had to arrange for a nurse to give me my jab there as I couldn't miss them. I have no idea why I was let out for the day when I was in isolation but I think the infection was showing signs of clearing up. The doctor had to see me and my Dad had to take me out of the ward to the outpatients clinic, which didn't make sense either.

The infection did eventually clear up and now I'm left with a lump inside the top part of my ear, you can't get a cotton bud or anything in it. But I have to say I would rather go through my spinal fushion or have a ceasarian ten times over than ever go through that pain ever again.

In 1981 I spent the whole of the summer in hospital having a Spinal Fusion. The operation was offered to me, it was life saving, if I hadn't had this surgery then I wouldn't be here now. My spine was curving at a fast rate and before the operation I had an 84 degree curve, which was pretty high. The fusion is a surgical technique in which one or more of the vertebrae of the spine are united then fused together so that motion no longer occurs between them. The body then heals the grafts over several months, similar to healing a fracture, which joins the vertebrae together so your spine doesn't move and so the curving stops. You then have a metal rod called a Harrington Rod screwed in to support your spine.

I knew that I needed this operation, there was no choice. So in the middle of June I was admitted to the Orthopedic Hospital in Stanmore for a long nine week stay. Stanmore was the best hospital I'd been in; it was like being out in the country and all the wards, outpatients and theatres were all separate little buildings. The buildings were so far apart you couldn't walk it; they even had a 'Horse Box' to transport people around, big enough to get two beds in. It was also easier for Mum and Dad to visit and there was also a place for parents to stay above the ward for as long as they needed too.

I had to go into hospital the week before my operation to have tests and prepare me. I was pretty used to going into hospital and it was a nice hospital as hospitals go. Able bodied girls would have to be on traction for weeks to stretch their backs before their fusions but my body wouldn't have taken that. On the Monday I had to see all the doctors, anaesthetist etc and I also had to spend 3 days in the Heart Hospital in London to have tests on my heart. An ambulance took me from Stanmore and I remember the ambulance driver pointing out Buckingham Palace and other landmarks. I didn't like this hospital, it was a very old and I had no visitors. I was 11yrs old and going to a hospital in London on my own, I was pretty brave.

I was back at Stanmore by the weekend ready for my operation on the Monday 29th June 1981, exactly a month before Charles and Diana's wedding. Mum was staying with me at the hospital for the whole week so at least I had my Mum there. It was scary as I had a long road to recovery ahead of me and a lot of discomfort. I was going to have to be laid flat on my back for a week, then plaster for six months and then a brace for another six months and then nothing!

On the morning of the operation my bed was wheeled into the Horse Box and I stayed in my wheelchair. Before going into theatre I was lifted onto my bed and left Mum and Dad. I remember lying there waiting ages for the anaesthetist, the nurses reassuring me everything was okay.

After a delay I was put to sleep and the whole operation took about eight hours. I remember coming out of the anaesthetic and lying on my front. My back was so painful; I was awake but couldn't move or make a sound and felt really scared. I thought they were operating on me still and hadn't realised I was awake! They turned me over onto my back and I could now speak, they must have been just putting the dressing on. You see they gave me just enough to knock me out. When I had my tests done on my heart they discovered one side of my heart was larger than the other. That's why there was a delay when I was waiting for the anaesthetist; they were trying to track down my Mum and Dad to see if they still wanted me to go through with the operation. The general anaesthetic could have been fatal and I could have died on the operating table.

Mum and Dad had to make the decision there and then, to carry on with the operation with a chance that I could die but if everything went okay I would have a longer life or to stop the surgery with a chance that I could die at an early age from illnesses such as a chest infection. There was no option really, I'm so glad they opted to go ahead or I may not be here now. They had no support from anyone either, they were just left to make this decision alone. That must have been awful, sat there waiting all day knowing that I could have died, I can't imagine what they went through.

"What would you have done?" My Dad has since said to me. I would have done exactly the same, the operation saved my life. Mum and Dad had no counselling and had to make that decision with out any help from the hospital. If it was now they would have had so much support, it must have been awful for them.

I was in intensive care for about four days and Mum was with me the whole time. I had to lie flat for a week and was turned every two hours to save getting bed sores. My back was very painful and they kept me dosed up with pain relief. When they were satisfied I was okay I was taken back to the ward. It was like I had been away forever. At least I could watch some TV now, which you would watch through a mirror you could pull down over your bed if you weren't actually laying the right way to see the TV screen.

In the middle of the second week I had a plaster cast done which supported the whole top half of me, it was like a plaster vest and I looked like an American footballer! It was uncomfortable having the plaster done, I had to lie on a thin bit of metal, and it wasn't pleasant. My new plaster vest had a hole in the back so they could still get to my large scar which needed dressing and a hole in the front for my boobs to grow, all the girls had the hole. Now the plaster was on I was allowed to finally sit up and to sit in my chair. I had to have the plaster cast on for six months, it was heavy and uncomfortable but you just got used to it. The worse bit was not being able to scratch your back, Mums knitting needles came in very handy.

Exactly a month after my operation Charles and Diana got married so the ward was Royal Wedding mad like the rest of the country. We made things, put decorations up and watched it on the TV at the bottom of the ward. The ward was so excited and it was a welcome distraction. I even kept scrap books; I loved anything to do with Diana and the Royal Wedding and remember having lots of magazines to look at in hospital.

I was eventually allowed home for a weekend after six weeks to get used to things again but had to go back for what we thought was just another week. My Dad came off his motorbike coming home from work one morning and broke his leg in two places. My poor Mum was going between Stanmore and the QEII in Welwyn and just couldn't cope with me coming out of hospital. Ben was even put with foster parents for a couple of weeks as Mum couldn't do it on her own. I eventually came out after nine weeks and I was straight back to school.

It was a relief to finally get the plaster off after six months and then I had a brace that I could take on and off. After another six months of wearing that I was brace free. The operation was a success; I could sit pretty straight with no backache now. Before my operation I had an 84% curve and they had got it down to 42%, so it was just half now which is pretty amazing. I don't get any back problems now just a bit uncomfortable with my coccyx if I'm sitting funny. I can't feel the metal rod and have yet to set off any alarms!

My brother also had the fusion a couple of years after me. A surgeon updated the way it was done and Ben was the first to have it done with that actual surgeon operating on him. Ben had no metal rod and the operation wasn't a success like mine as he started growing off of the top of his. They opened him up to correct the problem but his spine was that fused up they couldn't do anything and sewed him back up again. He ended up with quite a hump on his back and twisted, I think if that happened nowadays Mum and Dad could have probably sued.

That was really it as operations went. I had a nasty in-growing toe nail just before I started college and had to have it removed under local anaesthetic. I had a caesarean when I had my daughter and touch wood that's been it ……….. so far.

Chapter Four

This Used To Be My Playground

I started school in Stevenage in May 1974. It was a new school for physically handicapped children and was only built three years before. You see kids with a disability weren't able to go to comprehensive schools in those days, they didn't have the care and some schools just weren't accessible like they are now.

The school saw you right through your school years. They had a Nursery, Infants, Junior's and Senior's and now you can stay on in the 6th form. They had its 40th Birthday three years ago but the building is now sadly knocked down as they've built a brand new school in a different area of Stevenage. They held a reunion and we went along, it was quite sad knowing that the school I spent 14yrs of my life at would be demolished. Teachers were there who taught me and caring staff there who had looked after me, it's very sad to know I will probably never see those people again but then I thought that when I left 26 years ago. Let's hope there's a 50th Celebration, the building won't be around anymore but I'm sure we all will be!

The school was fantastic for it's time; I think there were only a couple of schools like this in the country. Your education was taken care of as well as your personal care. They had qualified Physiotherapists and Occupational Therapists. Toilet assistants were there during the day but they were known as the Welfare Ladies and there were qualified nursing staff. They also had a residential part of the school where pupils could stay Monday to Friday to give parents a break during the week. Both Ben and I eventually became residents. The care was provided by 'Houseparents' who you got really close too, I guess they were like your second parents. The residential part was known as the 'Flats' four separate flats containing four bedrooms, nine beds to a flat. Now apparently there are so many pupils wanting to stay they can only stay for two nights a week as there's not enough beds.

I started in the Nursery and my main teacher was Mrs Moore, a lovely lady who used to take me on holidays to her caravan in Norfolk with her husband, I have no idea why I was singled out but it's lovely to know she liked taking me away. The school even had its own caravan in Norfolk. It was a static caravan that was accessible and families with pupils at the school could book it for a week or two during the holidays.

My Mum and Dad didn't really want me to go to a school like this, they were worried that I would be held back and I kind of was. Before I started they spoke to the Headmaster and they were promised that my education wouldn't suffer, there was nothing wrong with my brain and academically I was very bright. The school had pupils with every physical handicap known, I actually hate that word 'Handicap', Disability is nicer. There were children with Spinal Bifida, Cerebral Palsy, Muscular Dystrophy and lots more; it was just a school for physical disabilities and not for children with learning difficulties. Though there were children there that were slower and learning was a struggle for them. My education did suffer because of this until I attended the local comprehensive school for my CSE's but I'll tell you about that later.

I was the only child with SMA right up until I was about 10, lots of boys with Muscular Dystrophy but no one with SMA. Not until a brother and sister from Watford started at the school. Catherine and Mr C (as I nickname him now) were just like Ben and I, the only difference was that they had a younger sister who was 'normal'. Ben and I used to hang around with Catherine and Mr C a lot; we would even stay with them sometimes. They had a massive bungalow and a van that could get two wheelchairs in it, which was amazing, we had nothing like this until Dad brought a transit van with a tail lift once Ben and I were too big to be lifted in and out of a car.

Catherine and I, although she was three years older than me, were best friends and I even had Mr C for a boyfriend when I was about 12. Catherine was the weaker one of the two just like Ben and me. She used to be off school with a lot of chest infections. We were inseparable and so alike. We loved music and we were always singing to songs with the words from Smash Hits and were always saying how we were going to start a band, we even tried writing songs. Catherine was always reading and writing, so clever. I was probably a little bit jealous as she was the girl who had everything, even the boy I fancied who is now in fact my husband. We used to laugh at the matron at school who had a fascination with our groins! We used to have 'bum cream' rubbed in every night so they didn't get sore and the matron would say in front of everybody "Catherine and Grace, I want to check your groins tonight!" yes, very embarrassing!

Catherine and I would have fun with the 'bum cream' though, when we were at her house we would get tubs of it and mix perfumes and other creams into it, put the new cream into her Dads miniature duty free bottles and say we had a new hand cream! We were always messing around like that and when she was off ill I used to really miss her. Catherine sadly died in the summer of 1983. Catherine's brother Mr C is now one of our closest friends. Mr C married a lady from Canada who I get on great with and she was a bridesmaid for me at my wedding, so we often have weekends together. We will go down to stay with them in Watford or they'll come up to Coventry.

I don't remember much about being in the Nursery and Infants. The memories I do have are of going on camping holidays, but I would stay in a caravan. I remember having a boyfriend called Sam, only because we shared a birthday, boyfriends aren't real when you're 7 are they? I used to go over and stay at Sam's house, take my Abba records over and we would even pretend we were getting married. That was the only boyfriend I had until Peter when I was about 10 or 11. Peter had Duchenne Muscular Dystrophy, he didn't live far from us and he was a couple of years older than me. Stevenage was about half an hour away and all the kids used to be picked up and be taken home by taxi and you would have the same taxi driver every day and your own wheelchair at school. At the end of school the front of the school would be full of taxi's waiting to take the kids home. Peter was in the same taxi as me as we were in the same area. Peter's Mum and Dad were also involved in the Muscular Dystrophy Campaign group in Hatfield. They were involved with the fund raising and they became good friends to Mum and Dad, they used to meet for a drink every week, such a lovely couple and good friends for years. I remember the four of them in fancy dress for a collection once, Dad was an Arab, Mum was Andy Pandy, Peter's Mum was a Looby Lou and I can't remember what Ben's Dad was. Peter and I would just sit holding hands or kiss now and again, but we were boyfriend and girlfriend although he was that shy he never used to talk to me!

As I'm on about boyfriends at school I might as well talk about the other ones too, there's not that many. You see at this school there wasn't much choice, the MD's, SMA's, Brittle Bones and a couple of other disabilities used to stick together. The only other boyfriend I had was Vincent, a boy with MD. I was a resident then and we used to go off and kiss in the Art Room, that's all we did, it was pretty much physically impossible to do anything else! The Resident department was a different part of the school so if you wanted to be on your own with a boy you would sneak off down to the classrooms. Between the classrooms there were toilets so we used to go down there and hope we weren't caught. I didn't though, I was too scared of being caught but I know others did, I only made it as far as the Art Room which wasn't that far away.

There was Mr C who I mentioned earlier and James, not at the same time! James was in the same class as me all the way from class 6 senior's right through to the end of school. We both ended up at college, although he started college a year earlier than me because I stayed on in the 6th form. James has Muscular Dystrophy but he's since found out he has another condition called Andersen- Tawil syndrome or known as Periodic Paralyses as well as the MD. He walked with crutches and I guess he was a bit of a catch at school. I was with him a lot of the time and I ended up having a massive crush on him, my first proper crush really, well apart from Nick Heyward from Haircut 100 and Jan James Vincent from Airwolf! Catherine went out with him and I was so jealous. He used to go and stay at her house but their relationship was always on and off, when they were off I used to think I had a chance. When we were 13 I finally got to 'go out' with him and we were together for couple of months. It didn't really work though and I ended up 'chucking' him, we were better off as friends......for now.

They were my only boyfriends, I didn't have as many as everybody else, and maybe I was just far too fussy then too! I now know that a lot of boys liked me but were too shy to admit it, college was the same, everybody always seemed to have boyfriends but I didn't. There was though this boy who would never leave me alone, he stalked me! I don't even know what was wrong with him; he could walk, had a big wobbly head, dribbled and had bad behavioural problems. His fascination for me started in the juniors, I used to make him his lemon curd sandwiches at tea time but his obsession with me got worse through school! He was always so naughty, always running away, always disrupting a lesson, I remember once he threw a rolling pin in Art at the art teacher. Sometimes it was funny and a distraction in class, he was so rude to the teachers if you could understand what he said! But there were a couple of times he used to try and kiss me, yuk, but there was nothing I could do about it, I couldn't push him away. Once I was waiting after school to be lifted into the taxi to go home, he came over and tried to snog me, it was disgusting, no one helped me! It still makes me cringe to this day, I was so upset and I never spoke to him again. I think he was moved to a school for naughty kids in the end so that they could handle him better.

The school always put on great Christmas plays. In the infants I was always cast as the Princess or Snow White, probably because of my very dark hair and being one of the few that could read out the lines properly. I remember being Snow White and having to pretend I was asleep in my chair and the prince had to kiss me to wake me up, not nice when the prince dribbled! The Senior Christmas plays were amazing. Our English teacher wrote them and they were funny, the headmaster would paint the scenery and the wings at the side and our Art Teacher would do the make-up. It was such a big production and would be on for two nights. I never had a big part in the senior plays, I was too shy. In Cinderella one year I was cast as a 'foghorn' for a scene at the Ball. I had to open my mouth and they would play a 'foghorn'. In Oliver I was one of the women in the work room and had one line and then one of the women in the pub singing

'Omm Pah Pah.' I didn't want big parts I used to get so nervous, in the Juniors we did The Tinderbox and I played the Queen, I was so nervous that I needed the toilet badly, so badly I was wriggling so I didn't pee myself. It was so bad that Dad was waiting to take me straight afterwards; I made it just in time!

I soon became a resident staying from Monday to Friday to give Mum and Dad a break. I shared a bedroom with Catherine and Kaz, Kaz had Cystic Fibrosis and she also sadly passed away the in the same year as Catherine. We would always hang around together, we were the main girls, we would always try and get on the same table at dinner time and tea time, and I used to have a panic if I didn't get to sit with the girls but we always managed to sit together. There were always five to a table and a member of staff to get the food from the hatch and eat with you. Dinner would be at 12.15pm and you would have your dinner and then go and 'play' for half an hour, lessons at 1.30pm. Tea was at 4.30pm so you had an hour before tea when school finished. I even had recorder lessons after school one night a week; every little girl takes up recorder lessons doesn't she?

We used to have trips out at night, shopping every Tuesday and late night shopping nights at Milton Keynes. We used to go to Wembley and see concerts, groups like Spandau Ballet and Depeche Mode. I used to get on great with most of the 'Houseparent's'. There were your favourite ones and then other ones you didn't like so much, the ones that would be rough putting you to bed. There were no hoists in those days so you were lifted, top and tail. A couple of times my legs were hurt being lifted into bed. Hoists are used now though, they're not allowed to lift, and at the reunion I was impressed to see a room full of them.

We used to have a Disco every single Thursday. Straight after tea we would get changed into our disco gear and do our make-up. Lots of lip gloss and glitter, boob tubes and knicker bocker trousers, we really went to town for the school discos! We didn't really dance, we would just sit in the corner, girls in one corner and the boys in another or when I was a lot younger we would just bomb around the hall, not dancing just driving around. The Christmas disco was the best one, we loved the discos!

We would have a school Sports Day at the end of the summer term just like other schools with activities like swimming, discus, slalom and javelin. Believe me a Cerebral Palsy or a blind child throwing a javelin isn't the safest of things! All the kids in electric chairs would compete in the slalom race, even though most of the chairs went at the same speed anyway, although missing the cones while you reversed was just pure skill! I used to hate swimming though, I guess it was good exercise; it was the whole getting undressed, getting out into the cold and getting dressed again. Once I was in the pool I was fine, I used to be able to walk as the water held you up. But as I got older and not as flexible I used to hate it, my periods were a godsend as it was a way of getting out of it. I used to have to have physio once or twice a week too. You got lifted down onto the mats and my legs would be stretched and my arms and hands, nobody liked physiotherapy but looking back it prevented my body getting stiff so quick, I carried on with my hands at college, physio was your own choice at college, but after a year I stopped going, I shouldn't have.

At 9 I moved into the Juniors Department, Class 4 and Class 5. I was always good at my work but shy, very shy and my shyness would be something that was always mentioned in my school reports or at parents evening; 'Grace hides her light under a bushel', 'Grace doesn't contribute to class discussions', 'Grace never looks into my eyes.' The last one was my English teacher who I used to have a crush on and so was shy because of that! I never used to put my hand up and only ever answered questions when directly spoken to. I'm not shy now, though I don't think I would put my hand up (not that I can get it up there) now in a big group, I can certainly make phone calls with no bother or speak to strangers, neither bother me and I will talk to anyone with a few wines down me!

I was good at English and I could write essays with no problem, I loved Art but I was rubbish at Maths. My Maths was poor all through school, I used to have to do the SMP (School Mathmatic Project) cards right up until I was ready to take my C.S.E's and then I was put in the bottom group. I haven't got the brain for it, maybe it was Lonsdale holding me back, but then again I was more interested in Art, you can't be good at everything. I much preferred being creative than working out boring sums and I liked writing. My Art teacher used to like having me in her class because I could actually draw and paint, some of the kids couldn't even pick up a paint brush, so I think it was nice for her to have a student she could really help.

I couldn't wait to move up to the senior part of the school; I was finally in the same part of the school as all my friends. Class 6 was tutored by a teacher who specialised in History. We would now go to various teachers for different subjects instead of one teacher that taught everything.

New teachers were always introducing something new to us. A new P.E teacher started and she suggested Wheelchair Dancing which we found funny at first and always got the giggles. We loved it though; we would even make up our own routines in the evenings. We used to just drive round in sync to the music, crossing over, going backward etc. The boys would find it highly amusing until they were roped into doing it too. We had about five dances in the end, one was to Shalamar's 'Night to Remember', another one the four of us girls made up to OMD's 'Maid of Orleans', a ribbon dance to OMD's 'Souvenir' and a stick dance to 'The Gay Gordon's'. We used to visit mainstream school's doing our show and we even had costumes! The girls wore green or light blue satin long skirts with a white frilly blouse; it was the time of the New Romantics so white frilly blouses were in. The boys wore satin shirts that matched our skirts and black trousers, they looked quite camp, very Strictly Come Dancing, all we needed were fake tans! I have to say though, our 'Maid of Orleans' routine was the show stopper!

Another teacher started the school who in fact became Deputy Head a few years later. He was in charge of all the video and TV equipment and got all the classes doing short films which we loved. My class did Strange Hill. Grange Hill was huge at the time so we did our own little take on it. James was Tucker Jenkins and 'the lemon curd sandwiches boy' Tuckers mate, my friend and I were Trisha and her friend. I really don't remember the story line but I remember trying to look hard with a bag on my shoulder, chewing gum. We were the only class to do an actual film; I would love to see that film now.

I went on a few holidays with the school. There would always be a foreign trip for the senior kids and I was chuffed when they chose me to go to Belgium. I was 13 and the number one single was Spandau Ballet's 'True', it always reminds me of that trip. We stayed in a school similar to ours but it was their school holidays so the kids were only there for one of the nights we were. My friend and I stayed in a bedroom together and I remember being so uncomfortable in bed, the school night nurse was trying to get me comfortable but she couldn't understand a word I was saying. All I knew in French was 'Merci', 'Bonjour' and the days of the week, only because I had a skirt with them all on when I was little. Once all the kids had gone on holiday we had the school to ourselves, our school would do a similar thing where a foreign school would stay with them. We went to Antwerp Zoo and Bruges but I have to say I didn't like it, too many cobbles and I hurt my ankle. The teacher pushing me slammed the front of my chair down going up a step, it was agony and after that I felt every single nasty cobble!

We went to Edinburgh for a week. We stayed at an accessible big mansion. Our English teacher I had a crush on, took us so I was happy! We had visits to Edinburgh Zoo, took a boat on Loch Katrine, a boat under the Severn Bridge, I really enjoyed it and funnily enough my future husband was on all of those trips with me.

I moved up a class every year and when I got to 13 I was due to start my C.S.E.'s. The Headmaster retired and female head took over and she believed in integration. She wanted to get children like myself out into proper main stream schools, mixing with able-bodied children. My brother Ben had been doing it for years. James, my friend Helen and I were the chosen 3, we had to choose 5 C.S.E.'s to take. I did Maths and English which were compulsory and chose History, Geography and Art, I had to do my Art at the disabled school as the Art block was up a flight of steps.

The Comprehensive was about 10 minutes away from the disabled school and had a good reputation. It was a school for 'normal' able bodied kids, we couldn't wait to attend although it was scary at the same time. I had been in this schools 'little bubble' since I was 4! We joined a few classes for the last term of the 3rd year before summer ready to start in the 4th year in September so that we weren't completely thrown into the deep end. Ben went to the same school but was in the 1st year and was doing really well. The 3 of us were in the same class for Maths and Geography but because we were all at different levels for English we were split up. I was put in the higher group, the group that would be an O'Level group the following year, I hated it. The other kids didn't speak to me, in fact my Art Teacher's daughter was in the same class but she didn't speak to me either. I loved Maths though, only because there was a gorgeous boy in the same class called Jake.

Oh my God, lots of 'normal boys', it was great! On went my blue eyeliner and mascara every day, my hair blow dried properly, I was like a kid in a sweet shop! Our Math's group was only small and so we got to know the other kids quite well. Jake had that cheeky look about him like my first crush Nick Heyward, he was gorgeous, and I had hated Maths before this, but not now! He was told that I fancied him and he made out he liked me too and came to Lonsdale on a few occasions to see me. We went to see Ghostbusters at the cinema and he tagged along. He sat in the seat in front of me on the school bus and this is when I had my first proper snog, yes he put his tongue in my mouth and I didn't know what to do! He also came to a Christmas school disco, we used to say to the other kids to come up and join us and so I invited Jake. I didn't know if he would come or not because I sent him a note. Yes I know, we couldn't send a text in those days, if you were too shy to ask them out face to face a friend would give them a note from you. So I sat by the front door of the school waiting for him, praying that he would turn up and he did! I couldn't believe it, he was lovely! I always used to look for his bag outside classrooms or the hall and sit near it knowing he would come along and pick it up and if he smiled I was in heaven! In the 4th year a friend 'asked him out' for me and he said yes, bit silly really because we never spoke and then I found out he was going out with a girl in the 2nd year too! That was really it, would love to know where he is now and whatever happened to him.

After the summer holidays we started at the school properly and started our C.S.E's. The three of us were together for Maths and Geography, Helen and I did History and we were all in different groups for English, me being in the top at C.S.E standard, not the o'level class. It was hard work at this new school, I've never worked so hard in my life but it was a great opportunity, finally the opportunity that my Mum and Dad 'had' been promised when I was 4 and started at Lonsdale. The Housemums weren't on duty till 7.30am in the morning so the Night nurse had to come in at 7am, wash me and dress me and then wait for the HM's to lift me in my chair and do the rest. We didn't have the big make-up routine young girls insist on doing now, but I always had my blue eyeliner and mascara on. My hair was cut short with a wedge and I had the rat's tail too which was bleached, my tail used to look nice when it was plaited with ribbon. I always had to have my hair blow dried in a certain way and only a couple of the HM's could manage it so I'd always ask one of them even if they weren't assigned to our block that week. I would have so much hairspray, my hair wouldn't move all day, that side flick had to be just right!

Ben and I were picked up by our normal taxi about 8.20am. I would get out of going to form before the morning lesson because I said I had to warm up first. I hated going to form; once again I didn't know anybody and all the kids just chatted amongst themselves. We used to have a room down by the Matrons to put our coats and lunch in. Matron and her assistant looked after us, they helped us with things like the toilet. We were there full time apart from doing my Art.

In the 5th year I had to really knuckle down and work, exams were soon upon us. We had different English and Maths teachers, my English teacher was the most amazing teacher, and his stories were always so interesting. I remember him doing a whole lesson on Jack the Ripper and it was fascinating. During the two years of our CSE English we had to read and do a review on six books from a big list, kids don't do this now, I've never known my daughter to come home with a proper novel for English, don't kids read anymore?! My six books were, if I can still remember and I still have my English folder somewhere, To Kill a Mocking Bird, West Side Story, To Sir with Love, Day of the Triffids, Kes and I really can't remember the other one. I loved English apart from when you had to give a talk. I hated speaking in class. For our Oral Exam we had to do a talk and read an extract from a book and so we had a practice run whilst we were videoed. I was shitting myself, absolutely dreading it. I chose to talk about me and my disability and I got so nervous I actually wee'd myself, nobody knew apart from Matron who had to ring Lonsdale to bring some clean clothes down. As for my talk, it went well, I don't know why I got myself into such a state. When we played the video back in class and the teacher said "Very well done Grace, you were actually looking into the camera", the boy behind the camera piped up. "That's because I was behind it Sir!" I replied and just went beetroot because he was one of the cuter boys in the class.

We sat our exams like everyone else but I think we may have been given an extra 15 minutes as we didn't write quite as quickly as the others. We had an exam for every subject apart from Art which was all just based on course work, my art teacher was so proud of my work that she had it all up on the wall in the school hall.

Most pupils went onto a college for the physically handicapped in Coventry. I was adamant I didn't want to go there, I wanted to go to a 'normal' college, and because I was now at an able bodied school I felt that going to this College would be taking a step backwards. So I had in my head to stay on in the 6th form at the comprehensive and still be a resident at the disabled school, I wasn't ready for college yet.

Once we had taken our exams we weren't needed back in school but I still went to school to stay for the week just to give Mum and Dad a break. I used to just stay up in the residents area, watch TV or read, although some of the teachers didn't like the fact that I wasn't doing 'anything practical' but at the end of the day I'd done my hard work and now it was a time to relax. I didn't want to be making more work at home and plus Ben was still going to school. This is when I found my fascination with Marilyn Monroe; I killed the time by reading books about her.

My grades were what I expected. I got a 5 in Maths, 3 in Geography and History, 2 in English and 1 in Art which I was really pleased about. Art was definitely my thing so I decided to do it at A Level in the 6th Form, I also did O'Level English, retook the Maths and a new subject, Psychology. I hated the 6th Form, nobody stayed on that I knew and so it was like starting all over again at the school, I was totally on my own. My brother was there to hang around with at lunchtimes but I wanted to make friends in the 6th Form. The 6th Form seemed so separate from the rest of the school. There was the main common room and it had its own canteen and lecture rooms. I had an area in one of the lecture rooms where I could study and do my Art. My Art teacher came to me now and I would do my Art lesson there doing the same as the other students who were doing the A Level Art. I used to go into the main common room sometimes but I was really shy and didn't really know anybody. A couple of the girls would help me with the lift at dinner time and at the end of the day. I would get invited to a couple of party's but that was about it. I wish I had just gone straight to college to be honest as the college in Coventry was pretty much the next step for most pupils leaving that school.

And that was my school education, as I said before the school in Stevenage was a huge part of my life and it was sad to finally leave it and move on. I was lucky to have a gone to a mainstream school and we opened it up for children after us.

James and I were invited back recently to look around the new school and talk to the kids that were soon leaving school. But society in general has had such a bad impact on the school. Don't get me wrong, the new school is amazing; it's massive with so much technology. There are ceiling hoists in every single room; even the lounges in the resident's rooms have them. Computers are at every desk in every class room and the bathrooms and toilets are equipped to make life easier. Even the lighting was top technology, you walked down the corridor and the lights came on, no switch to press.

There is so much Health and Safety, it's like the school has gone back 35 years and I was quite saddened by this. The kids can't go out and do anything without so many checks needing to be done weeks before any trip. They can't go out of the school grounds and it's a privilege to go out and mix with the kids from the school next door, what ever happened to the integration we started! I asked the kids if they went shopping or went to concerts and they said no. We were always going on trips or just popping to the shop over the road from the school. Even what they ate was strict; if they had a pudding at dinner time they weren't allowed one at tea, only fruit. They weren't allowed to have their bags on the back of their chairs just in case they tipped, ridiculous, I have loads of shopping bags on the back of me, I'm always loaded up!

I came away really wanting to help. They were lovely kids but have no clue about the real world out there. I thought I had been in the bubble when I left school but these kids really don't have a clue and it's so sad. I thought the whole idea of having two schools side by side was to integrate; hopefully this might happen in the future but I really don't think that's going to happen. The staff are so lovely and do an amazing job but it's just how society is now and there are restrictions in any school. There was talk of maybe James and I being on the Board of Governors but I think it would just frustrate me too much as I want the kids to be kids and have the experiences we had, but that's not going to happen.

It was weird how much I felt at home there even though it was a new building. I wish we lived closer as I think I would go down and spend more time with those kids and make a little bit of a difference. Another reason why I am writing this book, there is life after.

CHAPTER FIVE

Who's That Girl

College was just like the school; a college with all your care needs met. Coventry seemed a very long way from home but it was either stay at home and ware Mum and Dad out, go into a care home or go to college, there was really only one choice. Mr C, James and others from school were already there so at least I knew people.

I got my A Level in Art but I still didn't know what area of Art I wanted to go into so I applied to do the Arts Foundation Course. The AFC was a course that covered every aspect of Art from Fashion to Photography, Fine Art to Textiles. The course ran for a year and within that year you found what was your strength in art and I certainly did find out. It was the first year that the college offered it and it sounded perfect for me.

I had to firstly go for an interview in which I had to stay for the night at the college to see how I liked it. I loved it, I had my various interviews and was shown around the college and then James and Mr C took me down the pub which was literally opposite the college, this was to be my future local and there were to be many great drunken nights ahead.

The college was in Coventry about 15 minutes from the town centre and half an hour from Birmingham. The main part of the college had lots of lecture rooms, an Art/Photography room, a swimming pool, a Physiotherapy room and a huge Refectory where we ate and would have disco's and it was the main hub of the college where most students would gather. Two massive lifts that held about 4 wheelchairs would take you to the next level. Out from the Refectory was an outside walkway that took you down to any of the 3 residential blocks, one just for girls and the other 2 mixed. Adjoining the college was an able-bodied college, which had students from both colleges doing courses and vice versa, it was nice to have that mix of integrated students.

Each residential Block had their own team of carers and they would change them round a little bit every year. I was put on A Block, the block for girls and I was there for the whole 3 years. Before you started any lectures you had to start college a week earlier, this was to get you used to being away from home and help you to settle in. I was used to being away from home but not for a whole half a term, 6/7 weeks at a time. It was handy that I already knew a few people there so I wasn't completely on my own. You see James had come up to school on my last night there to see everyone and stayed, we ended up having a kiss and I was hoping something might come of it at college once I had started there but I was wrong. He'd been seeing a girl from college who also had SMA; he was with her throughout most of his time at college and eventually married her. My dreams of being with James were shattered once again.

Just before I started college in the September I went out and bought myself a portable TV, a hi fi and a mini kettle; I wanted to be as independent as I could and have all my comforts. There were about 38 bedrooms on one block, mostly single ones but new students would share one of the doubles. I guess so newbie's weren't on their own and having a single room was a status symbol for the second year students. I was given a double room and shared with a girl with Cerebral Palsy, she was really quiet and we had nothing in common. She got on really well with another girl so she ended up swapping rooms. For that first year I shared with another girl with CP called Cathy, Cathy was lovely, very lively and as for as sharing a room we got on fine.

The bedrooms contained a single bed, a wardrobe, a sink and a large desk with free Cable TV! The first week was great like a holiday. We could go down the pub and we could order take away. If you wanted a Chinese you would make the order and a taxi would deliver it to you, there was always a taxi driver wandering around the college with a Chinese take away in their hand. These days you would just find a Chinese that delivered. I never liked going in and eating in the Refectory at the beginning. You would have to queue and go through to get your dinner, I think I only ever did it once; someone would always get my dinner for me and they never minded.

The Care Staff were brilliant; it was like school, some you got on with better than others. In your first year you had to be on block by 11pm and then your second year by 12am but it depended on what care you needed, it was no good rolling in at nearly midnight when it took you a good twenty minutes to be put to bed. All students would take turns to do a 'Block check' to make sure all students were in and safe and you couldn't go to bed until all students were on block. The only time you were allowed out later was at weekends but you would have to get permission and get an official pass and also make sure the night staff could put you to bed. The day staff worked till midnight and then the night staff took over until 7am. Each student had a personal carer assigned to them so if you had any problems then you could talk to them; mine was a lovely lady I got on well with.

The first week was soon over and lectures started, I'd forgotten I was actually there to study. There were only four of us on my Arts Foundation Course. A girl who had Spina Bifida, an Indian lad called who had Muscular Dystrophy, I had a crush on him a little bit through out college and a guy from Liverpool with Spina Bifida who was amazing at Art. The girl on my course and I were inseparable during the day but we didn't see much of each other out of lecture time as we both hung around with other people.

We had our own work stations in the Art Room; Foundation was more about you finding things to work on and left to your own devices, not needing a teacher to stand over you telling you what to do, holding your hand. Our main lecturer was a lady who had taught Art at the college for years and another lecturer from Nuneaton. I found him so hard to please, he was into fine art, throwing some paint at a canvas or finding something out of a skip for inspiration wasn't my thing but this was what the Foundation Course was all about, finding out what you were good at and what you weren't. This was the very first year the AFC was introduced at this college and so we were the guinea pigs.

We did most areas of Art. We had Photography every week with a great lecturer who everybody loved. History of Art and Life Drawing, I remember our first life drawing class, none of us had ever done it before and so we had the giggles. A lady used to go around all the colleges working as a life model, she was in her 40's, small and must have been used to students with the giggles but after a while you just got used to it and didn't think anything of it. Thankfully it wasn't a man standing there with nothing on with his bits for everyone to see!

I did struggle with the course; it was hard for me as I didn't have the imagination to do things off my own back. I didn't sketch all the time in my rough book like I should have done. That part of Art just didn't interest me and I was worried about still not knowing what area to go into. It wasn't until nearer the end of the course that I found out what area I wanted to go into.

I had a large circle of friends from the beginning and I soon got out of my shyness, I had to. My confidence grew, by the end of my first year I was a blonde with big scrunched hair, black eyeliner and red lipstick but that was the fashion then, I really wanted to look like Kim Wilde. Everyone seemed to be going out with each other and I hoped I would get lucky at the discos and it never happened but then there wasn't really anyone that I fancied, well not until a guy called Tom came along.

Tom was what everyone called an 'outsider', people use to come and hang out with us, and this is how I met Susan who almost became my sister in law. I can't even recall how Tom ended up going down to the college; think he just went along with a mate one day. He'd been out with one of the carer's daughters who had nothing nice to say about him and eventually banned him from the blocks which I never understood at the time, now I know! He was a bad boy and I liked that and plus I loved the attention. He was funny and had the most amazing blue eyes, I've always fallen for a funny character and I guess this was my first proper experience of blokes.

Tom and I got together one drunken night, we were fine for a couple of weeks but he suddenly stopped going down the college as much. There were no mobile phones back then so it was just a case of hoping he would turn up some evenings and when he did I would be on cloud nine once again. I remember him meeting Mum and Dad when they had brought me back up after a holiday; I've never heard him go so quiet. I soon learnt that Tom was seeing other girls when I was away at home so we ended. I think this was the first time my heart had been broken, I was stupid to think that I was the only girl he was seeing. Things were never fully over though; he would say to my friends he still liked me. There were rumours that he was going to suggest we get engaged, but that never happened thank God! Tom was around for the next twenty years of my life, until he destroyed our friendship for good.

My first year flew by and by the end of it I knew what I wanted to do in art. The Art teacher gave me a project to redesign an off licence logo and I really enjoyed doing it. Graphic Design was now what I wanted to do; I had a flare for it. There was a B-Tec Diploma Course at a Technical college in town so I applied. This meant I could still stay at the disabled college for my care and travel out every day to do my course, like I did at school. I had an interview, I didn't have that much Graphics work in my portfolio but they offered me a place.

When I started back for my second year at the college I had my own room, had Marilyn posters and even a Marilyn clock up, it was very me. My brother started in my second year and he also did the Arts Foundation Course. I did see quite a lot of him, in fact there were a lot of really cool students starting that year. It wasn't until my second year that I felt I really had fitted in and made close friends.

I was really nervous about starting my Graphics course, I was now completely on my own. The disabled college would pay for a taxi to pick me up at around 8.30am and take me to the college and then pick me up at 4.30pm, it was the same driver every day and so I was fine in a taxi on my own, no way I could do it now as I need holding onto. The only problem was the toilet. The disabled college had to send someone to come and take me to the toilet but it was so much hassle to go I just didn't bother and held it in all day. I held it from 7am in the morning until when I got back just before 5pm and if the care staff were busy just before tea I would wait until after that, it wasn't good for me but I didn't have much choice. I would have a cup of tea in the morning and then that would be it until I had been to the toilet in the evening, sometimes I didn't even eat in the day. The Technical College was a big old building and had a couple of lifts. I would be dropped off by the side entrance as the main door had steps and then went round to the reception and they would take me up in the lift as I couldn't do it myself. At the end of the day someone in my class would take me back down.

There were two classrooms, one for the first year and one for the second year that were next door to each other. There were two main lecturers. Ours was the head Graphics teacher and she saw us through both years. There were about fourteen of us in the group, most were straight from school. The class was all boys apart from one other girl who was always making little models, she was so clever and a woman that was a mature student, all the rest were boys. We all had a big desk each but they were really low so mine had been raised on blocks so I could work comfortably at it. They had never had someone like me on the course before so it was a learning curve for everyone. I wasn't able to use the light boxes. A Light Box is basically a box with a light so you can easily trace work or lettering through the papers. So they brought a little portable one so that I could use it at my desk. I didn't even know about light boxes, my work was pretty bad and not like everyone else's until I discovered it. I got on great with the guy sat beside me and he was always really helpful.

On the course I had to do Photography and as I couldn't physically do much myself i.e. develop prints, the lady who was meant to come in to take me to the toilet would do photography with me on a Monday morning. We had to do History of Art in the theatre room I found it hard staying awake and often felt like I was dozing off. Marketing was boring too and didn't do well on that in my final marks. I enjoyed Computer Graphics; I guess it was something I could easily do. I liked the Computer Graphics lecturer, a gay guy who was very down to earth. We also had a normal art class, which involved drawing still life and the idea was to include your work into your design work. But mostly our lessons were with Judith who taught us the basic design stuff like Typography, Page Layout, and Packaging amongst other things.

I did find it tiring, it was long days and I found it hard keeping up with the homework, plus college had a lot of distractions. I wanted to sit with the others in the Refectory, not be stuck in my bedroom doing work but looking back I wish I had worked harder, I had an opportunity to do really well but college life took over more than it should have done.

My designs did get better; I loved the final result of my work once it had been mounted and displayed nicely. At the start of every term we were given our main project like having to totally revamp a leaflet or a page in a magazine. Your ideas were really important and we had to show how we got to our final idea. We had to design artwork for art week at the college which I really enjoyed. We had to come up with the poster, t-shirt, leaflet, tickets and I thought my final work was good. In the second year we had to change the whole design of a business and I chose to do a wedding shop in Coventry. I messed around with designs and came up with the final one putting it on a letterhead, envelope, and complimentary slip and once again I loved the final result. It was really satisfying looking through your portfolio and having your work all neat in plastic sheets. I don't like mess now, maybe that's why I went into graphics and not fine art as graphics was always neat.

In my second year we used to hang around with a lot of outsiders and this is how I met Susan, without Susan in my life I wouldn't have gone down the road I did. Susan started coming down the college with a girl called Kerry and we instantly clicked, she was like the little sister I had never had. She was still at school, so probably only about 15 at the time, lived not far from the college with her younger brother and her Mum and Dad. We were inseparable back then, she was seeing a guy called Nigel who also used to come down to the college and his brother was seeing one of my other friends so we just used to all hang around together.

There were some amazing characters at college. You see, we can take the piss out of each other but no one else can, that's why I've taken the mickey when talking about school, it's just how we addressed each other. We had a girl who was named 'The Flying Foetus', she was tiny and had Brittle Bones and one day she banged into something and flew out of her chair so the name stuck. There was 'Marg' who had permanently widespread legs (you can work that one out) and many more students with nicknames. We had 'Spook a Spack Week', where basically you would make a CP jump by throwing your tray down loudly. One day the boys even moved the tables around in the refectory so when the blind boy went for breakfast he had no idea of the lay out and kept driving into tables, very cruel but funny!

I loved my time at the disabled college once the first year was over. I even had a boyfriend for a short time, it might have only been 3 weeks but my God did this guy make an impact. Neil was another outsider and used to come down with his mate. Once again another funny character, wasn't the best looking of blokes, always reminded me of Ricky from Eastenders and the lead singer of The Housemartins, he had the long floppy hair. He made me laugh so much and when I heard he fancied me I was really flattered.

It was quite funny how we got together; we were down the local pub The Woodies. We'd been flirting all night and when I left the pub he stopped me in the car park, we kissed and we didn't want to leave each other. I kept telling him that I had to go as I needed to be back before at least 11.30pm and so he unlocked my wheels so that I couldn't go anywhere. He kept saying "My Nan lives in a bungalow, you can stay there", if only it was that easy.

After lots of protesting and kissing I spotted one of the care staff marching up the hill looking for me. Oh shit! I was really late in and the care staff were waiting to put me to bed, oh well, it wasn't like that happened all the time, I was normally a good girl.

I was so happy for the 3 weeks we were together, all we did was sit in my bedroom kissing, I loved his company and he was all I could think about. Everybody used to laugh at him as he would always have red lipstick round his mouth after a good kissing session. It ended as quick as it started though, Neil stopped coming down to the college and I spoke to his mate and he told me he had got back with his ex. I was heartbroken; my chair wasn't working at the time and so I was stuck in a manual chair. I had to know what was going on, so Susan pushed me to his Nan's bungalow and there he told me to my face that it was over and he was back with his ex. It took me a while to get over him and I never saw much of him again.

He's on my Facebook but I've never actually spoken to him. That was it through college, just the two guys.

My social life at college was amazing. We were always going to concerts. I saw people like Whitney Houston, Heart, T'Pau, Bros, Erasure. We would go clubbing, I remember one night club had steps and so we would get the bouncers to carry us up, it was like we didn't have any fear then, no way I would do that now. There was a disco most weekends and we would always make the effort and dress up. I used to get so drunk, many a time I've had my wheels unlocked and pushed down to the block with my head in a cup throwing up. We would drink loads, always sending people up the off licence for a bottle of Thunderbirds or Smirnoff. Sometimes you just didn't want the weekends to end, but it was back to the grind stone every Monday morning.

I loved my third year at college, the second year of my Graphics course. I really got into the whole Graphics world and my work got much better. I loved the end result, seeing your final piece mounted and placed in your Portfolio. At the end of the year we had an end of year course exhibition where we had to put up our best pieces of work and I was proud of what I had achieved. I didn't think I was up to Degree standards though and a degree was a lot of theory which I wasn't great at. I wish I had of tried now, who knows where I would be now if I had carried on. I passed my Graphics, I didn't get a high mark but I had a B-Tec behind me. I didn't carry it on and that's one of my biggest regrets as I decided to have a rest and have a year out and do nothing, maybe do a small bit of graphics work but that didn't happen. Maybe I should have studied something else and I could have ended up having a good job, but I was crap at Maths and my passion was Art. I still do the odd bit now on the computer, for example I did all my wedding invitations and designed the whole look for our wedding which I was really pleased with. I can knock a poster up with no problem and I enjoy doing it, maybe I could have gone into Computer Graphics and been very good at it but I'll never know now.

I had to decide what I wanted to do once I had left college. All I knew was that I wanted to stay in Coventry and wasn't ready to continue my education so I decided to take a year out.

One of the students at the college also with SMA had a bed-sit not far away. He had a car that he could drive up in to and had a carer driving the car which I thought was amazing. I wanted to live like that and have a car like him. I'd never seen a car like this, Mum and Dad had the big transit van for Ben and I, nothing like this. So the plan was once I'd left college to find a place to rent, find a couple of live in carers and eventually get a car and go back to studying. I wanted to be independent but it was all so much harder than I would ever imagine.

Chapter Six

I'm So Stupid

I left college in June 1990 and to be honest I didn't want to leave. I didn't want to leave my friends; I had such a great group of friends now. Also my care was all there and I didn't have to worry about it. The plan was that a house would be found to rent during the summer holidays and then I would move back up to Coventry at the end of August. My brother was at college for another year doing the second year of his Graphic Design course and so Coventry was always going to be my best option.

Charlie, one of the lads on my Graphic Course wanted to rent a house too once we left college and so we got talking. We thought it would be great if we could find a house and he would have a room like a shared house and he was cute! My friend Kerry, one of the outsiders, wanted to be my carer; she left school and wanted to go straight into looking after me. We also got Jenny to work for me who was the daughter of the Principal at the disabled college. They knew they wouldn't be on a lot of money to start off with but they would be living in the house, didn't have to pay any bills, rent or food, it was all down to me and in the end I was bled dry. Mum and Dad helped me out by paying the bond and Housing Benefit took awhile to sort out. I also applied for the Independent Living Fund which would pay for my care but this would also take awhile to sort out.

Charlie found a house to rent in Earlsdon, which wasn't far away from where the other guy with SMA lived. The house was near to town, easy for shopping and nights out. There were two rooms downstairs so one would be my bedroom and the other the living room. It had a long kitchen and a downstairs bathroom off the kitchen. Two bedrooms up stairs so Kerry and Jenny had a room and an attic space which Charlie had to himself. It was furnished, which was handy although the furniture wasn't nice, all old fashioned but it was a start. There was a big step into the front door and my Dad made me ramps, and a step down into the kitchen but this was just for now, I wanted to get myself on the housing list as soon as I could.

The first month was like a party. We would drink and smoke joints all night, then sleep all day. It was the freedom to do exactly what you wanted with no one to answer to. It was no way to live but we thought it was great. Drugs were going on, one night a lad got a load of coke out and put it on a mirror but I only ever smoked Draw or Weed then.

Money was very tight; I had to pay for everything apart from Charlie's part of the rent and had to give Jenny and Kerry £30 a week wages just until the ILF had sorted my care money out. Bearing in mind this was 1990 so £30 was a lot more money back then.

I still went down to the college some evenings, but only when I could afford the taxi to get down there. I still saw Susan and Nigel who I spent a lot of time with at college, but things were slowly changing in the house, I wasn't happy. Arguments started going on between Charlie and the girls and one weekend when Charlie was away they decided to do graffiti on his bedroom wall, very grown up! Of course when Charlie came back he went mad, so I was in the middle of the arguments. He came and said that he really couldn't live there anymore, I was great to live with but he wasn't prepared to put up with the girls anymore, which was fair enough and I didn't blame him. So Charlie moved out. Jenny started having a boyfriend and other friends round a lot and the house just became a doss house. I had nothing in my life to get up for anymore; I wished I had stayed on at college.

Mine, Kerry and Jenny's relationship got really strained, lots of petty arguments. One minute Kerry and Jenny were best of mates and I was the bitch or Kerry would be in a mood with Jenny and I was in the middle, it was a nightmare. I started going down to the college more to spend time with my brother and just to get out and away from them, some nights I just didn't want to go home. The vibes in the house were horrible; I didn't ever expect it to be like this. I gave the girls a weekend off and I went to stay at Susan's and had a lovely weekend. I didn't want the weekend to end, I felt sick when I thought about going back to that house with them again.

Things came to ahead. I can't remember exactly what was said but there was an argument between the girls and me and I remember Jenny saying to me when I was in bed "If you weren't in a wheelchair I would of hit you" Jenny had a bit of a reputation as quite a hard girl, a daddy's girl that always got her own way and very spoilt. I was a little scared and I didn't want them in my house or looking after me anymore, I'd had enough. I went down to the college and got talking to one of the carers who had looked after me when I was there; Laura had always been one of my favourites. I was really upset and said how I didn't want to go home. That night she offered to come over and put me to bed so I didn't have to face them. I was in a manual wheelchair as my electric wasn't working and Susan put me into the taxi and the girls would get me out the other end. The girls wheeled me into the living room, didn't even take my coat off, left me and went upstairs. Laura turned up about half an hour later with her friend, put me to bed and stayed with me for a little while. As soon as Laura left the girls came down the stairs having a go at me. "What are you involving her for?!" they asked.

Mum and Dad were coming up and staying that weekend and I told Jenny and Kerry they could have another weekend off. Susan stayed with me and looked after me and that weekend I told my Mum and Dad how unhappy I was and that I wasn't getting looked after properly. Mum always brings up how she caught me trying to wash my hands with wipes as I hadn't been able to have a soak in the bath, I'd had strip washes and washed my hair in the bathroom sink but that's all I could have. It broke my Mum's heart seeing me trying to get clean like that. I didn't want the girls anywhere near me and the college offered to take me in for a week just so I could get more care sorted, they were so helpful. Dad phoned both the girls and told them both that he knew what was going on and they were not to return to the house in Earlsdon.

At the college I was put on C Block, the block Ben was on. They gave me a bath and it was heaven just being able to have a nice soak. I never really had anything to do with the girls again, I'm not just blaming them but the three of us just didn't work, we were all really young and it's a big wide world out there. Standing on your own two 'wheels' is much harder than you think as I learnt again and again for more years to come.

Susan couldn't bear to see me go into any home or respite and I only had one week at the college to sort myself out. So it was decided that Susan would move in with me, she already had a job so I needed care in the day whilst Susan was at work. Susan had a knack of getting me into bed on her own; she would lift my top half over onto the bed, lie me down and then bring my legs over, if only it was that easy now. Home Help had been arranged to come in at 9am every morning to get me up and then once in the afternoon to take me for a wee and then Susan was home in the evening to cook my tea and put me to bed. After my week at the college I went back to the house, Dad came up, got the house straight again after the girls has trashed it i.e. the graffiti and I was finally happy.

I had the same ladies in from Home Help, who were lovely; I got on so well with them. Nigel was always at the house and he'd help Susan out with my care, I even got baths as they were able to lift me in, I was never embarrassed about Nigel seeing me naked because it was just Nigel. In the end Nigel moved in with us, it just seemed the right thing to do as he was always there anyway.

Tom started coming round at the end of the year and all my feelings for him came back. This is when I lost my virginity to him, I was almost 21. To be honest it was like he took that and ran off again and believe me, my first time wasn't pleasant and wasn't how I had imagined it, it hurt and was far from romantic. He was out of my life again as quickly as he came into it and it was years before I saw him again.

To help with the rent the lady from Home Help said she had a couple of student friends that were looking for a room to rent and I had the attic and the other bedroom just sitting there empty. So her two male friends moved in. It was really strange having two strangers in the house, one of them just kept himself to himself and the other one was very geeky and quiet, wouldn't hurt a fly. He used to sit down in the living room sometimes with us, he did try to fit in with us, bless him. Once again it kicked off, they didn't get on with Susan and Nigel and I was in the middle, again. There was a big argument between Susan and the quiet one and then a big row with Nigel and the other guy. Nigel had locked him out and so he ended up smashing the back door window. So in the end they left the house and it was back to us three again.

My 21st came, we hired a room and a few of my friends from college came and by this time I had started seeing Susan's brother, who was younger than me, Daniel which I'll go into in the next chapter. It was nothing official but we were sometimes seeing each other.

Susan, Nigel and I had so much fun. We were always off to the bingo or clubbing. Susan and I were both into music and loved singing and we were always singing into microphones and trying duets, we sounded pretty good sometimes. We even had a day in a proper recording studio. Her Uncle was in the Coventry band King who had the hit 'Love and Pride' back in the early 80's and he said we could record a track with us. Susan had written a song when she was at school called 'Ulterior Motives' and so he played around with that. Her Uncle was so clever, just added keyboards and other sounds and then it was our turn to do the vocals. It was meant to be both of us but I was just pushed to the backing vocals and it was mostly Susan which I was a bit pissed off at. The end result was pretty good even though you could hardly hear me, maybe that's why it was good; I have no idea what ever happened to the tape.

I even bought a car. My first car was a two door Austin Metro and I had it sprayed bright red. I brought a two door as the doors were bigger and Nigel had more room to lift me in and out. I would have loved a car I could just drive into in my wheelchair but Mobility didn't do them yet, if you wanted a car like that then you would have to buy one yourself. I've had a car for years now, I started off with a Fiat that looked like a Pope mobile back in 1995, Renault Kangoo's and now I have a really nice Peugeot that looks like a proper big family car. We were always out in that little red car; we even went to Great Yarmouth and Hull.

Things got a little bit strained between Susan, Nigel and I sometimes, I was always the gooseberry and things got quite awkward sometimes. Some nights they would get comfy on the sofa, throw a quilt over themselves and it was obvious things were going on under there, yes, definitely awkward, so I would just go to bed with my personal stereo so I couldn't hear what they were up to.

We swore the house was haunted too. I would do Ouija boards and one night the table tipped and the lights flickered, really scary. Also Susan was putting me to bed one night and the door was slightly open and someone walked past, you could just see a shadow in the hinge of the door. We ended up all sleeping in the room downstairs as I didn't want to sleep on my own. This couldn't carry on as we all needed our own space. My name was down on the Housing list and a flat came up in a bad part of Coventry and there was no way I was living there for my own safety. We even looked at flats and houses to rent as we didn't want to stay in that house anymore. We looked at a couple of places but the bedrooms just weren't big enough.

My care money had now come through and Susan and Nigel got a massive back pay which they put down for a deposit on a maisonette which was just around the corner from Susan's Mum and Dad's. It was exactly what we wanted, a huge living room with two biggish bedrooms all on one level but a small bathroom, though I could still get in to be lifted in the bath. I still kept myself on the housing list as one day I wanted a bungalow or flat of my own, I couldn't stay with Nigel and Susan forever.

We moved out of my house in the autumn of 1991, I was only there a year but it felt like so much longer. Nigel had started looking after my brother Ben too as he had left college now and he also wanted to stay in Coventry. He ended up moving in and we shared a bedroom, I was almost 22 and was now sharing a bedroom with my brother. He got a job designing T-shirts in a building that was on the grounds of the college but needed somewhere to live and needed care. At the time it made sense that he moved in and Nigel was Ben's paid carer.

Susan and Nigel were onto a good thing, they had care money from me every month and care money from Ben. They also had a lot of money off us for bills and food. For example Susan was always on the phone to her Mum even though she only lived over the road, but we still split the phone bill four ways even though Ben and I hardly used the phone. Don't get me wrong, the both of them helped me out loads and if it wasn't for them I would have probably been put in a home or something, but the pair of them started getting quite greedy. Bringing in 2k a month back in 1992 was a lot of money. If Ben wanted to use a night's care money for someone else to look after him Nigel would get really funny about it. Ben used to go into town a lot and Nigel started giving him a time to come in, he had to come back for 1am or the door would be locked. We were young adults who could do whatever we wanted within reason, if Ben wanted to come in at 4am then tough. That was Nigel's job; we felt like kids sometimes, they called the shots just because we lived in their flat.

They sorted out the PAYE to pay their tax and national insurance but I found out that they weren't paying it. I ended up having a huge tax bill a year later once I took over the money as they weren't working for me anymore and I was the one that was liable to pay it back. I eventually paid it all back, I had no choice.

I even had a dog from the RSPCA, an Alsatian cross called Jay. Susan and Nigel decided to get a dog of their own too once we had moved. Both dogs were never taken out for walks apart from when Susan's Dad took them over to the woods with their own dogs. When the dogs were left on their own in the flat they would wreck the place because they needed more attention. It got so bad that one day Susan took both the dogs out and came back with their collars. She had them both put down, didn't even discuss it with me, I was fuming! She could have had them re-homed but no, instead had them both put to sleep which didn't make sense. Why did the vets put down two healthy dogs? With the right family they would have made great pets. She must have made up some over exaggerated story! What really pissed me off was once I had left and moved into my own bungalow they got yet another dog!

Ben moved out first, he had a good social life and he ended up sharing a maisonette with a girl called Karen who he had met when he was out drinking. Karen was his main carer and Nigel used to do a couple of days a week for Ben too but Nigel started really taking the piss. A few things happened like Ben's rent going missing one month and Nigel started signing up to things like Britannia music using Ben's address, Ben knew nothing about it. Things got really bad between Nigel and me too, he just got nasty and greedy. Susan and Nigel got married in the summer of 1994 and I was originally going to be one of Susan's bridesmaids, I was even measured up for my bridesmaid dress but because Nigel threw a paddy and fell out with me so I didn't end up being one. I was fired from my chief bridesmaid roll; in hindsight he did me a favour as burnt orange really wasn't my colour. I think Nigel changed Susan a lot; things could have turned out so different if they hadn't got too big for their boots and got greedy.

A housing association bungalow came up; a new estate was being built in another part of Coventry which was a known area for prostitution and drugs. It was brand new but only had one bedroom which was fairly big, a large living room with patio doors into the garden and a decent size kitchen and bathroom. I took it on as it was better than living with Susan and Nigel forever and I finally had my own place at last. Susan was going to come over and look after me whilst Nigel was at Ben's but things went from bad to worse with them and Nigel was sacked.

Nigel and Susan ended up divorcing after a couple of years. Susan fell in love with a woman and left Nigel. I only heard stuff through Daniel, Susan's brother; I never spoke to Susan again which was a shame as we were so close. Sadly in 1999 Susan took her own life, I think there were lots of reasons mainly a stressful relationship with her girlfriend and she too started taking Speed. I went to see her in the chapel of rest and I wish I hadn't.

Nigel also passed away a few years ago from Cancer. We'd made up and spoke now and again, plus his sister worked for me for a number of years. He never had a good word to say about Susan and wished he never married her but they were young. Nigel lost his fight with Cancer on a plane coming back from Spain, he knew he hadn't got long and tried to squeeze a holiday in and almost did.

Looking back now, I'm the only one left apart from Daniel and he got what he deserved in the end, I'm a big believer in Karma! Sometimes I think I'm just a curse or maybe God really is looking down on me and sorts the people that hurt me, well, apart from my brother of course. There was a third party between Susan and I which did end up ruining any relationship we ever had, her brother Daniel.

Chapter Seven

Rescue Me

This part of my life was horrific, very bad times. I still beat myself up now, I can't believe I let someone treat me so badly, I would never let that happen now, no man will ever treat me like that again! It's mentally scarred me for life, maybe I should have got counselling but I thought I would be okay.

I met Daniel through Susan. He was her younger brother and younger than me. He always looked and acted older and I was attracted to him from day one. Well, maybe not day one because the first time I met him he wanted to show me his dinosaurs when Susan took me round her house to meet her parents. He was 12 and looking back it's unbelievable to think that that boy would be the father to my baby and in my life forever.

Daniel used to come round and see Susan and I guess it was somewhere to 'doss', there was something between us and Susan used to be a little matchmaker. Looking back now I wouldn't have wanted my best friend who was older and my little brother getting together, that's just wrong.

The first time something happened between us was the night before Valentines Day 1991, he slept in my bed and we just kissed. A couple of days later we were 'going out' with each other but we just kept it quiet. He looked so much older than he was, he always has done.

Our secret came out at my big 21st birthday party. Nobody was really bothered though, his parents still didn't know so we were able to still see each other in secret. We finished after a couple of months, but it was always on and off.

Susan and Nigel were always trying to fix me up with someone else during that time. There was a stage when they tried fixing me up with Nigel's younger brother, John who was my age but nothing happened there, he was too quiet for me anyway. There was also Alex, Nigel's best mate and something did actually happen with him, well just a kiss and other things on a couple of occasions, I think we tried to have sex once but we struggled physically. It wasn't happening which pissed us both off, when it comes to a guy, physically, sometimes it doesn't work, now I know it's not essential and there will always be a way you can do it and if the guy is patient and is caring enough you'll find a way. It's great when you meet someone and you find a way that's comfortable and doesn't hurt you. I liked Alex a lot, he got a job in Hull and moved away, we spoke a lot on the phone and we wrote but that was it. Susan and I even went up to Hull for a night, off we went like Thelma and Louise on our adventure. She couldn't even lift me in and out of the car; we had to make sure there was someone there at either end.

Daniel and I had feelings for each other and they grew stronger over the next year and a half. When I was offered the bungalow in April 94, my first proper home, he would come and stay. If he got into a bit of bother and had arguments with his Dad he would come round. Daniel started looking after me and moved in when mine and Susan's friendship ended, it just seemed like the next step. He was always a massive flirt though; he couldn't help but flirt with any woman or girl that he came into contact with making me paranoid all the time. He invited some women and their daughters who he worked with at the bakery to our house warming; he flirted with all of them. It kicked off, my friends weren't having any of it and they told him so, he was out of order big time. He'd flirt with my friends and my brothers friends, he just couldn't help himself.

I loved him and I wanted to make this work and I believed he loved me. We had fun, I think because he was younger than me and I was immature at times we kind of met in the middle, I could be really silly with him. By this time his Mum and Dad knew, we met his Mum in town on her lunch break and she made it clear that she didn't like the idea of us being together but she would put up with it, well at least that was something.

Not long after we moved in together I miscarried, it was only a very early one and I didn't even know I was pregnant. I was a few weeks late and had a period that was a lot heavier than normal and the doctor said he thought it was a very early miscarriage.

I really can't pinpoint when the violence and drugs started, I think it was going on for most of the three and half years we were together and it was worse when he got in with the wrong crowd. I'd had the odd joint at college and sent to the principals office as I'd been caught. The Principal wanted to know where the students were getting their 'wacky backy' and it was his daughter getting it for us. He said it wouldn't go any further and the staff were on the alert for anymore drug taking but that didn't stop anybody. I remember having a spliff with one of the care assistants in their flat, there was a lot of it going on. One night I got really stoned and had to face the senior nurse going back onto Block, trying to look normal is very hard when the slightest thing has you in fits of giggles. We would either smoke it in the Principal's house when he was out, yes right under his nose or somewhere outside away from anyone.

Daniel used to smoke draw quite a lot through the day, I didn't smoke it with him that much, and I didn't even like the smell. I used to have a joss stick burning or make him go outside as I couldn't stand it.

It was the Speed, Whiz whatever you want to call it that was our down fall, maybe not mine so much but definitely Daniel's. He used to be so nice one day, really helpful and loving but the next day he'd be in a foul lazy mood and would sleep and sleep, so heavily that I wouldn't be able to wake him. If I did manage to wake him he would shout at me for waking him, telling me to shut up and leave him alone, all I probably wanted was a cup of tea or the toilet. There would be nights where I would just have to stay up in my chair because I couldn't wake him. I'd be sat crying, pleading with him to put me to bed but I just got shouted at. In bed sometimes he

Grace Saunders

would roll over and the quilt would go with him and I had nothing over me. I'd be lying there cold and pleading with him to cover me up but again I was just shouted at and told to shut up.

The rows were really bad, screaming at each other. If I was able I would have just got out of the house, gone for a walk or for a drive but I was stuck and felt so trapped. I remember his mate was over and we sat at the table playing a game and we started rowing again, over what I can't remember. He picked up a cup of tea and threw it over me, I screamed as it was hot and he pulled my t-shirt off me as soon as he realised what he'd done.

Daniel was my sole carer; it was a lot for a young lad to take on and I wish things had been different and I had got another carer. The care money wasn't great in those days so you couldn't really have other people doing it because the pay was poor and plus we were stubborn. Well, in the beginning stubborn but in the end we had no spare money as everything would go out on bills and Daniel's 'tick bill' (a 'tick bill' is the money you owe your dealer at the end of the month because you've had your drugs lent to you) that he used to run up every month. There would hardly be any money left for me, Daniel's tick bills would came first or there would be people at the door. We even had a dealers gear stashed in the attic at our second bungalow. The deal was, we had it hidden at ours and Daniel would get free weed or draw. Where was my favour? All I had was the worry of knowing it was up there. I was shitting myself and after a week I told them that I wasn't having that shit in my house, it was too risky and it was gone.

Daniel admitted to me that he was taking Speed and to be honest, I liked him more on that as he did more, he was a far nicer person. He was the messiest person; I think that's where our daughter gets it from because I'm certainly not like that. Our kitchen was disgusting, he didn't do the washing up and dirty plates would be stacked up for days. At one time I think Daniel's uncle who sometimes used to stay with us counted twenty empty milk bottles because Daniel couldn't be arsed to put them out for the milkman. The floors would be dirty, no washing done for a week or more and I used to get so frustrated because I hated living like that. I was bought up properly, in a clean home and I couldn't live like that. I think that's where a lot of the arguments would stem from.

Our rows would end up physical. Something in the bungalow would always get broken; we had no pictures up on the wall in the end because Daniel would smash them. He would punch walls leaving massive holes. Doors would be put through and we'd have to replace them, I think we went through two lots of tables and chairs because his fist would go through them. Every argument I would think 'oh God, what on earth is going to be smashed this time?' It didn't just stop at our home and belongings; he started to get more physical with me.

He would be out for longer periods with his mates leaving me on my own for hours at a time. I don't mind my own company but I started getting cabin fever. I needed the toilet or a drink, he would come home and we would argue. He would be off out again and we would argue. He started hitting me around the head which bloody well hurt; it was so hard one day that I hyperventilated. I used to sob my heart out screaming at him, he couldn't treat me this way.

We used to stay up all night taking speed and be up until the next night and then sleep all day, that's how our life was. Daniel would put a small spoon full in my cup of tea and that would be us up and wide awake for hours. My brother and his carers would come round and we would all be taking it, up all night, we hated it when the sun came up and morning was here. So much so that one morning we covered all the windows up so that no sunlight could filter through and it still felt like night time so that we could carry on with our speed taking. It was awful when I look back now. I liked staying up with him taking speed, it was the only time we spent together because he was out any other time and he was nice. We'd play on the Sega, listening to the local radio and just be stupid together. I spent my whole time doing puzzle books; I would go through piles of them. When you're on speed you have to be doing something with your hands, there were no computers so it was crosswords. I look back now and can't believe how I used to keep myself occupied and we had no Sky!

He did hurt me quite badly on a few occasions. He threw an aerosol can at my foot once, it broke the skin badly and I couldn't move it for a couple of days, couldn't even have the duvet over it because it was so painful and yes, he was very sorry. Things would be thrown at me, he would lift the back of my chair up and rattle me about, my brother was there when he was doing it once and he yelled at him to leave me alone.

Spit, I hate people spitting but it got to that too. I had no way of getting physical with him and yes I shamefully admit I spat in his face when he was in mine. But he would do it back double, getting it up from the bottom of his throat to spit into my face and hair, awful. And yes, I would scream at him but just through sheer frustration. When he was nice he was lovely, he would lift me onto the toilet and into bed, and he had back problems so it wasn't doing him any good.

I would always yell at him to leave when we were arguing, he would but then be back an hour later. We would make up, be okay for a little while and then it would start all over again. He would be in a state like me, he said I used to ram at him with my footplates, maybe I did, but not without a lot of provoking and who cares, the guy was hitting me round the head for God's sake!

It got so bad that I took about twelve Co- Proxomols one night while he was out. I just sat taking them, I knew that twelve wouldn't have killed me, just make me ill, but I wanted Daniel to realise how low I was. I phoned him and told him what I had done and he came straight home, made me take some Speed and I went back out with him clubbing. I know, bizarre! I was okay, just very tired when we got home. I was just screaming out to him, he couldn't treat me like this!

He started hanging around with this blind guy, this guy used to click his fingers and Daniel would go running. We were the only ones with a car and Daniel and people took advantage, if people wanted a lift Daniel would take them, if I wanted anything I didn't get it or I had to wait.

We lived about fifteen minutes from where Daniel was brought up and he used to go over there quite a lot, I couldn't stand the people he was hanging around with. He started hanging around with this couple with a few young kids and one on the way. They lived in a scruffy flat and it was an open house to anyone. She was a dealer and so Daniel was going there getting his gear. Her fella was okay, I got on fine with him and I tried my best to get on with her for Daniel but I didn't like them, they were rough and they were coming between Daniel and me. Again, he would run them around and do anything for them but for me, no. They had two great kids though, 9 and 7, I loved having them to stay and taking them out.

Mandy didn't have long left of her pregnancy and Daniel couldn't run around after her enough, it was hurtful to see what he would do for another woman but not for me. Daniel was even on call to drive her to the hospital when she went into labour, yep, drop everything just so long as Mandy was ok. He also got in with the big dealer round the area, giving him lifts everywhere; Daniel's head was so far up this guy's arse it was unreal. Whenever they popped into the bungalow with Daniel they would be polite with me, I think they probably felt quite sorry for me and knew how unfair and selfish he was but didn't say anything. The blind guy is the step dad of a carer I have now and he says now how selfish Daniel was and how he didn't look after me properly.

Something happened unexpected though that summer and I hoped that it would change Daniel, I fell pregnant.

CHAPTER EIGHT

Little Star

Finding out I was pregnant was a big shock. Daniel and I hadn't used any contraception since he moved in with me and we thought there was something medically wrong with one of us and we weren't able to have children naturally. My period was two weeks late, which wasn't like me as I was as regular as clockwork

Daniel got a pregnancy test from the chemist, I did the test and he dropped it in, I think it took an hour. He came back and said "Hi Mummy", he knew before I did that I was pregnant.

It just didn't feel real, I don't think any woman believes it until you actually see your baby on the screen when you have your first scan. I was scared, excited, happy, worried, so many emotions, Oh my God! I was going to be a Mum. Was I going to be able to carry the baby okay? What about the birth? How the hell was I going to give birth? What ever I was faced with I was determined to do it, I was going to have this baby! Daniel was pleased too, I was hoping this would be the thing that sorted him out, to be a proper family. We were buying bibs, bottles and dummy's straight away, you have to buy something don't you?

Then there was the worry of the baby having SMA too, I was always told it wasn't hereditary, so I wasn't worrying that much. I did ask a Dr a few years before if it was possible for me to have a baby and she said no. I now know the baby would be a carrier of the SMA gene and would have an SMA child themselves if they had a baby with another SMA carrier, which would be rare anyway. I don't think I could have coped with a child with SMA, it sounds hypocritical and we certainly wouldn't be able to give a child with a disability the attention it would need. I had a good upbringing etc but I don't think I'd want to see my child go through the operations, physiotherapy, falls out of wheelchairs that I had. My Mum always said "If we had known you would have ended up like this we wouldn't have had you", which sounds really harsh and quite mean but I agree with her, it's not the easiest thing bringing up one disabled child let alone two.

I made an appointment at the doctors where I would see the midwife regularly and they made a hospital appointment for me. I had to go down to the local hospital for blood tests which are always quite traumatic. It's always really hard finding a vein because I can't straighten my arm enough and typically, my first blood test went missing so I had to go through it all again. After I had Erin I had to have a blood test in my foot which was just as painful as I have bad circulation in my feet. It was either my foot or my groin because they couldn't find any more veins in my arm. The hospital still have problems trying to find veins, probably due to my hands being a little chunkier and plus I can't stretch my arms out.

My first antenatal was exciting; it just felt more real then. They gave me my due date which was 14th May 1996 but the baby would be born earlier than that because I wouldn't be able to carry to full term. They gave me a scan but as I was only 12 weeks they couldn't see anything because the foetus was too small. They said I could have a camera inside me or I could wait a few more weeks, I chose to wait as I doubt there was much to see anyway and I didn't fancy the camera thing.

Everybody was so excited for me, my Mum and Dad had always assumed that they would never have grandchildren, Ben had no regular girlfriend, and it would have been easier for him to father a child than for me to have one. He was excited about being an uncle so this baby growing inside of me was going to be very special to a lot of people.

My next antenatal was at 16 weeks. I met the doctor who would deliver my baby, a very nice lady; I knew I was going to be in safe hands. She went through everything with me, my background, the SMA, the scare over my heart that we had when I had my spinal fusion. I would be having a caesarean section and put to sleep, there was no way I would be able to have an epidural because of my back. I wouldn't be awake to see my baby being born and Daniel wouldn't be allowed in the theatre room either. The baby would be in the Special Care Baby Unit (SCBU for short) because of being born prematurely. The doctor advised me to go as far as I could with the pregnancy, the longer I went the better and healthier for the baby.

I met my midwife in late October. She was lovely, you could imagine her living on her own with lots of cats, and I knew I'd be able to talk to her about any problems. I felt fine, I was sick just the once and that would be the only time throughout the pregnancy. I felt very tired though and this was only the start.

I had my next scan just before Christmas at 21 weeks, the doctor herself did it. The baby was doing fine, growing well and I could see it so much clearer now. We could see its head really well and it was sucking its thumb, it was hard to believe that in about three months I would be having this baby and the pregnancy would be all over with.

We went down to my Mum and Dads for Christmas. I was starting to get a little uncomfortable all ready, I had really bad heartburn and backache and this was only going to get worse. As I wasn't mobile I also had to start injections to thin my blood called Clexane. I had to have one a day and be injected into my tummy by Daniel, the nurse showed him how to do it and it was fine. Sometimes they would really hurt and other times I didn't feel a thing, I would end up with lots of bruising all over my tummy and I got quite worried as the baby got bigger about sticking needles in there just in case it could feel it on the other side, I know there's a lot to get through before you get to the baby but it was always in the back of my mind. I never drank or smoked, I remember trying to have a Baileys, it was Christmas and I wanted to have at least one drink but everything gave me heartburn so I just didn't bother which wasn't a bad thing.

Laying in bed was getting more and more uncomfortable, I mainly laid on my side but when I rolled over it felt like the baby was falling out of my womb, a very strange feeling. So I had to lay on my back all the time and that got uncomfortable. I had to lie on a massive cushion and then have lots of pillows under my legs. We even got a portable TV in the bedroom so at least I could lie and watch TV if I needed to lie down. Some nights I didn't get much sleep at all so I was prescribed sleeping tablets, but I was only to have one if I was really desperate, because too many would harm the baby. They would knock me out for about three hours and then I was wide awake.

I started getting pains in my chest, because the baby was pushing up. Because of my scoliosis the baby was quite squashed, I even used to worry that the baby would come out squashed, but I was worrying over nothing. The backache was getting worse, I would have a cushion behind me in my chair but sometimes I just couldn't get comfortable.

I had another scan in mid January at 5 1/2 months. Women don't normally have this many scans, unless they have an underlying medical problem anyway. You have to drink lots of water before you have your scan which was a problem for me; I never drink a lot when I'm out because it's so physically difficult going to the toilet. So I would have maybe one little plastic cup of water and hoped you could still see the baby clearly enough, it was either that or be busting for a wee and not being able to go until I got home. We asked what sex the baby was and she said she thought it was a girl, but not to go out buying everything pink just yet. I really didn't mind what I had, as long it was healthy, we were having a little girl. Would she look more like me than Daniel? Would she be blonde like him when he was little or really dark like me? I had a feeling she was going to have lots of hair from the heartburn I'd been having.

I can't remember how far gone I was when I felt the baby move for the first time but it's such a lovely feeling. It's hard to explain, it just feels like a movement in your tummy that you've never felt before. The baby was really active all throughout my pregnancy; even now Erin fidgets and can't sit through a film, but when you felt that movement you knew everything was okay.

I'd stopped going out now. I remember going out with my brother to a nightclub and I think I only stayed for about an hour. I felt frumpy, fat, uncomfortable and just wanted to go home. You couldn't really see that I was pregnant because I wore leggings and baggy jumpers, plus you couldn't see a lot because I was sitting. It did my head in, all I wanted to do was show my bump off and look as pregnant as possible. If I had gone full term I don't think I would have been that big anyway.

My next scan was 6 weeks before I had the baby, it was definitely a little girl, and I'd got used to the fact that I was having a little girl now. I was in tears a lot of the time, probably a mixture of things, hormones, being uncomfortable; being scared of what was ahead for me and of course the problems with Daniel.

I was also worried about not having enough room; we lived in a one bedroom bungalow. When I accepted the bungalow I really didn't think that I would need the extra room for a baby just yet, if at all. Our bedroom was reasonably sized so we would manage for now; there was no need to get a cot just yet anyway. She would be okay in a Moses basket for now, someone we knew was selling one, it was perfect, had the embroidery anglaise, so pretty. Mum and Dad bought the pushchair which had the changing bag, cosy toes, and parasol with it. We picked up things like the sterilizer and changing mat out of the paper so we were pretty much sorted for her arrival.

At the beginning of March I just wanted the baby out, I didn't know how much longer I could go on. I was getting heavier and heavier and Daniel was struggling to lift me now, I'm a dead wait anyway but how the hell he used to lift me at 7 months pregnant I will never know. I even had an electric bath seat given to me from the occupational therapists because Daniel couldn't lift me down into a bath or out again and I couldn't sit in the bath now without support.

I went to see the hospital for the last time to have a check up with the doctor and she told me to go for at least another 3 weeks, oh no, another 3 weeks!? But I knew I had to for my little girl, she might be so small that she might not survive, so I had to go as far as I could so she had some sort of chance of being a healthy baby. It really didn't matter that I was uncomfortable, my baby came first.

I was booked in to have the baby on Monday 25th March. I had to go into hospital on the Sunday night ready for my caesarean the next morning, finally I had a date. I was scared but I wanted these 3 weeks to go as quickly as possible. I also had to start having steroid injections to make the baby's lungs grow more. I had to have four injections, the first two spread over the weekend 2 weeks before the birth and then the other two the following weekend. A district nurse would pop in and do them. I had them in my bottom and they were quite painful, I felt like a pin cushion what with the Clexane jabs I was having too.

I just wanted everything over with by now. I had my final visit with the midwife; she came out to see me at home to make things easier. I told her that I was scared, it was natural to be scared and she said she would come and pop in on me at the hospital when I'd had the baby.

At last the day had come when I went into hospital. I had a room to myself which I was glad about and Daniel also had a bed in the room so he could stay with me, he only stayed with me that night. We were taken down to SCBU to be shown round so we knew what to expect and where the baby would be for the next couple of weeks at least. There were two main rooms, one for really small babies and the other one for babies that have been moved from the first room who are doing well and ready to go home. The babies were tiny; you could just about see them in the incubators, so much machinery keeping these little babies alive. There was one with tiny kind of black toes like matchsticks and it was quite upsetting to see them that small, but these were babies that had been born at 27 weeks or more. The staff were really nice and they said that they would see my baby tomorrow and not to worry.

We went back to the ward and I was hooked up to the machine to hear the baby's heartbeat which was really strong. We kept losing the connection though, because I couldn't hold it hard enough onto my tummy so Daniel had to keep pressing for me.

Daniel and I couldn't sleep that night, it was the first night I'd slept without my big cushion and I wasn't comfortable. I must have got some sleep though as the morning soon came, I was on Nil by mouth so no breakfast for me. Daniel put me in the bath; he had to bring my bath chair in for me. I had to put one of those horrible gowns on, which gaped at the back, sitting down has it's bonus's sometimes, at least you couldn't see my bum!

I drove down in my wheelchair to the labour ward while a porter pushed my bed down and I was taken into a room. A midwife came in and had a chat with us, she said they would shave my pubic area at the top and put a catheter in for me which freaked me out more than having the baby! It was a good idea though as it would mean I wouldn't have to be moved onto a bedpan after my operation because it would be too uncomfortable for me, with a bag and catheter I could go to the toilet and nobody would even know I was doing it. I really didn't fancy having it inserted while I was awake so she said they would do it once I was asleep.

Daniel lifted me onto my bed, the doctor came to say hi and that she would see me soon and also my Mum and Dad arrived. The nurse shaved me under my tummy and Daniel got into his gown, he was going to have to come into the operating theatre with me to lift me onto the table, once I was asleep he would have to leave, but at least he would be with me until I went to sleep.

The porter and midwife collected me, pushed my bed into theatre, such a horrible feeling looking up at the ceiling as you're wheeled down knowing that you'll be put to sleep soon and that when you woke up you were going to be in pain but at least I would have my baby and it would all be over with. Mum and Dad kissed me goodbye and I was taken into theatre.

The anaesthetist took awhile to get the needle into my hand ready for my drip. I would have a morphine drip put in, it was a button I would press to give me a shot of morphine when I was in pain. I thought he was going to break my fingers, he really hurt my hand by the way he was squeezing it. The worse thing was the gas which I hate. It's not so bad being put to sleep with an injection, but I hated having gas. I asked if I could count to ten which I had always done when I'd had an anaesthetic. All I remember is going into that dream like state and looking at Daniel, I got scared and apparently I was trying to pull at his gown and they had to stop. It upset Daniel to see me like that and he said he would never love anyone else as much as he loved me at the point, I doubt if that still stands but it was a lovely thing to say at the time. They took the gas mask off me and tried again, this time it worked.

* * *

Erin was born at 10.23am weighing 4lb 5oz and was beautiful. I'd done it and I was finally a Mum! We liked the name Erin from the beginning.

I was so sore; it felt like my stomach had been ripped out. Everything was a haze that day, I was so tired, and all I wanted to do was sleep. Everybody was congratulating me and said everything had gone very well and Erin was in the incubator on SCBU. I remember my Dad saying "She's a lovely little thing Grace",

He was a very proud Granddad. I wondered what my baby looked like, I wanted to see her; all I had was a Polaroid photo taken when she was just an hour old. She was tiny, had tubes coming out of her little body and wore a woolly pink hat to stop any heat coming out of her head, she was perfect, it's amazing how you instantly have that love for someone that you don't even know. My Dad said that they were in the corridor when the incubator was rushed passed them as soon as she was born so they had briefly seen her.

The pain was quite bad and I kept trying to push my morphine button but I was too weak to push it so my Mum was pressing it for me, they told her that she shouldn't be doing it but there was no way I could press it myself. I had a dressing that covered quite a bit of my tummy and I had a 'classical cut' which went from under my belly button downwards instead of across under your tummy, they didn't want it getting infected because of me sitting. I also had my 'piss bag', it kept filling up and I didn't even know I was weeing, such a good idea, if it wasn't for a big tube hanging down from inside me and big bag stuck on the side of my chair everywhere I went I think I would have had one permanently, it would of made life a lot easier for me!

I stayed down on the labour ward all day, sleeping on and off, the midwife coming every so often to check my temperature and blood pressure. Daniel kept coming and going, he was allowed to spend a little bit of time with Erin, he was getting in that bonding before me but I was so tired I really didn't care at the time, I just wanted to sleep.

Mum made me have little sips of water and opened cards and presents with me, I couldn't do anything, I had no strength at all. Somebody bought me one of those balloons with 'Baby Girl' on it and there were lots of cards from people.

Anne, Daniel's mum came down on her own; she'd seen Erin and said she was beautiful. She sat with me for a little while but I didn't really say much to her as I could hardly keep my eyes open let alone have a conversation, which I felt bad about but I'm sure she understood.

They kept me on the labour ward for longer than they usually would because I had very high blood pressure so that had to be kept an eye on before I could go back to the ward. After a few hours it calmed down and the midwife kept saying "Do you want to see your baby yet?" and I just kept saying "No, I'm too tired…I can't keep my eyes open for long enough"

They decided I could go back up to the ward around 6pmish and they would push my bed down to SCBU on the way so I could see Erin for the first time. They couldn't get my bed into where Erin actually was so they lifted her up at the window so I could see. Wow, that was my baby, she was so small, but I would have to wait a few days until I could hold her. I felt very proud of myself and I would now have to leave her again as I had to go back to the ward. Goodnight baby, Mummy will be back real soon to give you lots of hugs and kisses.

I was pushed up to the ward and back into the room I had spent the night before in. All my familiar things were in the room; my Mum had put my cards up and flowers in a vase so it would feel as homely as possible.

A male midwife introduced himself and said that he would be looking after me over night. He had to keep pressing my morphine button for me once my Mum and Dad had gone. Everybody went home and I was left to sleep, sleep and think about my new baby girl. I hoped she was okay down there without me, I knew she was in safe hands. She was a pretty good weight considering she was 7 weeks early and if she was anything like her Mum she was going to be a little fighter.

I had quite an uncomfortable night, I couldn't for the life of me push that stupid button, and in the end they took the morphine drip out of my hand. I had morphine injections in my bottom every few hours which was so much better; I was in a lot less pain, why didn't they just do that in the first place? They left me alone most of that Tuesday so I could rest, Daniel came in and to be honest I felt so alone that week, stuck in that hospital bed wanting to be with my baby. They say that a caesarean birth isn't the same as actually giving birth, one minute you're pregnant and the next your not, your body hasn't gone through the labour so it's a bit of a shock to it. Most women can hold their babies pretty much straight away but I couldn't and it was killing me.

It got to Wednesday night and I was so desperate to hold my baby, I told one of the nurses and she arranged for me to go down to SCBU with Daniel, it was the middle of the night and I was high on morphine but at least I would finally get to hold my baby. Daniel sat me in my chair, I tried to drive it myself but I was just too weak. He had to push me, 'piss bag' hooked onto the side of my chair, my wee for all the world to see, my big fluffy teddy bear slippers and my Mummy nightie on and I was ready to properly meet my daughter.

A nurse lifted the side of the incubator down, wrapped her up and passed her to me; I was finally holding my baby. She was tiny, so cute and all I could do was stare at her. The nurse took a Polaroid of the three of us and wrote on it 'first cuddle with Mum and Dad', I had two photos now that I could keep with me when I was upstairs on the ward, it wasn't far but it seemed such a long way. I didn't want to put her back but we weren't allowed to keep her out for too long just in case she got cold. Daniel put her back and changed her nappy, he did pretty well considering she was so small. She was still wearing hospital clothes because our own clothes were slightly too big for her, still she'd soon grow into them.

All week I would go and sit with her when I could, either holding her or just watching her sleep in the incubator. When I got my strength back a little bit I was able to sit and feed her which took forever but I couldn't do the winding bit. I remember sitting with her one afternoon and I felt wet, I automatically thought Erin had wee'd on me but didn't know how when she had a nappy on, it was actually milk coming out of my breast, I'd totally forgotten about that because I didn't give birth and I didn't breast feed. I totally forgot that I was still going to produce milk so I wore breast pads for a few days. My hormones were also going mad, I remember feeling so down, Daniel didn't spend that much time with me, he was too busy getting out of his face with his so called mates, I know you have to go out and 'wet the baby's head' but he over did it slightly, I felt so alone.

By the Friday I was staying up longer in my chair, I was off the morphine and having normal pain killers every four hours. My catheter came out too, I hadn't been for a number two all week and whilst I was sat on the toilet the nurse took it out which didn't hurt, I was going to miss it! Daniel brought the portable TV in because I was so bored.

On the Sunday afternoon, Mum, Dad, Ben and his girlfriend came to see Erin, who was now 6 days old. We had a side room on SCBU where we could sit with her, those couple of hours were lovely and I just wanted to go home now. My stitches came out that night, which hurt but it was so much more comfortable without them. I saw the doctor on the Monday morning and I told her I really wanted to go home now, I could rest better there and have a little more company. She said she would discharge me if I was totally sure and I was okay. The only thing that did bother me was leaving Erin in the hospital, going home without my baby was heartbreaking but SCBU said we could go in whenever we wanted to night or day.

It was good to be home though, we'd had a new double bed delivered whilst I was in hospital and Daniel hadn't even bothered putting it together, I wanted to lie down and had to wait for him to put it together, he'd had all week and I wasn't impressed! I wanted a nice welcome home but all I got was a messy house and no bed, I was straight out of hospital and still very tender. What made it worse was having no baby to bring home; my heart just ached for her.

For the next week we were backwards and forward to the hospital, I was trying to be there as much as I could, even if it meant Daniel dropping me off. One night we went to see Trainspotting which I absolutely hated, the whole thing with drugs was just too close to home. There was a scene where a baby dies because drugs were left around and it really upset me, I can't watch that film now. To top it off Daniel dropped an 'E', I was so angry! After the film we went to the hospital to see Erin and he was just sat there out of his face trying to act normal.

During the second week Erin was moved into the next room in SCBU, she was in the normal trolley they put babies in. They called it 'the bread bin' she was feeding well and gaining weight and after 2 weeks we could take her home. It was a scary thought, she was finally our responsibility, not the hospitals, and we were going to be totally on our own now.

We had her dressed in her new outfit and little coat, put her in her car seat, which she looked tiny in, thanked and said goodbye to the nurses. First stop was Anne and John's and then home. It was just so strange to have her home, I think we just put the car seat on the sofa and stared at her thinking 'what do we do now?'

It was hard work for Daniel; he had to sort a baby out now as well as me. She slept brilliantly though, she would wake for her bottle about 6 in the morning and Daniel would lie her in my arms, I would feed her and we'd end up falling asleep. She was such a good baby, I think it was her instinct to be good because of me which helped a lot.

Going out was a bit of an ordeal, not just loading me into the car but Erin and her pushchair too. We'd go into town and people would stop us all the time because she was so small and cute. It was a great feeling knowing people admired us and were interested.

We had to go to the clinic at the doctors every few weeks to get her weighed and checked out by the Health Visitor and there was never a problem. For a premature baby she was doing brilliantly! Apart from the obvious problems, I loved being pregnant and if I'd been able bodied I would have sailed through my pregnancy; I know I didn't have to deal with giving birth but I think my pregnancy would have been fine.

I had done it, I had the baby I had been longing for and I felt very proud! I've actually researched on a SMA chat site called SMASpace. I wanted to know how many Spinal Muscular Atrophy women in the world have had babies and there aren't that many. Most of the Mums have SMA III, a few with SMA II Intermediate, the same as me and what really amazes me; a woman with SMA I! I struggled so it shocks me how these women have carried a child, the giving birth bit I understand because of the Caesarean but these women are a lot weaker and have more of a curved spine so they're bent over more.

I did find out that there are two Mums in Russia with my type of SMA. There's a lady in Canada who I had the pleasure to chat to briefly on Facebook. This lady is an award winning radio producer for the Canadian Broadcasting Corporation and has apparently blogged and been the focus of several 'radio essays' on the subject of giving birth and being a Mum with SMA. When I looked through her photo's I was amazed at how she coped as she looked a lot weaker than I, but then again I did have Erin 18 years ago when I was a lot stronger than I am today. There is a girl I went to college with who I lost contact with over the years, she had the same SMA as me and has a little girl. I'm slowly hearing about more SMA Mums as I join more and more groups on the internet. It makes me feel even more blessed and lucky to have Erin as she is such a special gift.

I've received messages from parents who have children with SMA and they are so encouraged by my story. They have hope that one day their daughter may be able to have a child. Medicine is coming on all the time and the care and treatment will be more advanced than 18 years ago and will be even better in the future. It gives me great satisfaction knowing that I can help other women with SMA who are worried about carrying a child and giving birth, that's why I wanted to write this book. I want women to think 'Wow, if she can do it then so can I!'

CHAPTER NINE

The Beast Within

Life didn't get any easier, things gradually got worse. Daniel was going out for hours on end leaving me on my own with Erin; I couldn't do anything for her. The options were leaving me without my baby for hours because he would take her with him or the two of us would be left at home. I didn't like the places he was taking her, didn't want him meeting up with drug dealers with her in tow.

I was taking speed again now I'd had the baby, and the drugs got worse. The first time I took an Acid Tab I was spiked, Daniel spiked me. He was taking them with his mate, another mate I didn't like, and wanted me to try one and I kept saying no! One night his mate was over with his girlfriend and they thought it would be highly amusing to spike us both. It takes awhile to come up so I was fine and then suddenly I started to feel strange, colours were brighter, everything just looked different, and yes I was tripping. Daniel was in my face, I couldn't handle it, suddenly all I wanted was my own space and I started freaking out, why was I feeling like this? Daniel came clean and told me he'd dropped a tab in my drink and to be honest as soon as I knew what was going on I was okay and when I had calmed down I actually liked the feeling.

We dropped more acid together, I guess it was a way of escaping and it also meant he was around more, wherever drugs were there was Daniel. It was either do drugs with him or be on my own for hours on end. I was so unhappy, I had a beautiful baby girl but my life was shit. When Mum and Dad came up for the day I hid everything from them, I was fine. When we watch the old video's taken from back then I'm not the woman I am now, I look ill and my eyes are dead. It was always a panic whenever Mum and Dad came up, I would worry the bungalow would be a mess, my Mum is the cleanest person I know so I didn't want her to find fault in anything. It would always be a big rush to get the bungalow clean, tidy and the washing done and not lying on the bedroom floor. It was a lot for Daniel to do on his own but he didn't make things easy for himself, never tidied up when he made a mess so it was always one big clear up.

We put in for a move and a 2 bedroomed bungalow came up just over the road from us, I was hoping for a better area but the bungalow they were offering us was nearer the prostitutes and high rise flats. We had a look at the bungalow and it was quite big, a huge living room, 2 big bedrooms, a bathroom with bath and shower, a separate toilet, a big laundry room but quite a small kitchen. There was a yard out the back, not much of a garden but it was a sun trap when the sun was there.

We accepted the bungalow and very slowly moved our stuff in, slowly because it was when Daniel could be bothered. You have two weeks to move from one property to another and I think he left it till the last minute to do anything. I remember him moving our bed first and having it in the living room for a couple of nights, nothing was organised at all. It was just a case of moving our stuff over bit by bit. We ordered carpets and had points with the council to order wallpaper, paint etc. but the bungalow never felt like home; I hated it and was even more scared when I was left on my own.

The dealer helped Daniel lay the carpet in the living room and I think Daniel did the carpets in the bedrooms, but to be honest it was a blur then. It was the end of November and I really wanted everywhere nice for Christmas but it would be the worst Christmas of my life, we had finally had enough and grew even further apart.

Daniel was going out for longer periods and sometimes all night. I couldn't get myself to the toilet and I would have to go into the bathroom and wee on the floor, how humiliating. I used to have to do it at the old place if I couldn't get there and was desperate. I would stuff toilet paper between my legs, try and wee slowly so it absorbed it and then when I'd done pull it out and put the paper down the toilet, sometimes it wouldn't hold it all and there would be a puddle on the floor so I would mop it up with my helping hand. I felt dirty and ashamed but what could I do? Daniel would put me in the bath when he came in or gave me a wash on the bed. One time I was desperate for a number two, I seriously couldn't hold it in, I'd rang Daniel but he was either busy or wouldn't answer the phone. Sitting in your own poo is the worst, why was I letting this happen, how did it come to this? I was scared though, I couldn't just walk out but if I was able too I would have got Erin and walked a long time ago. Who was going to look after me? What would happen to Erin? Would Social Services take her off me? Would she go off and live with Daniel? I didn't know where to turn.

Erin was old enough to stand in her walker by this time, so Daniel would put her in that so at least I could kind of get to her. She would whizz around in that and then fall asleep with her head on the table, bless her. If she wasn't in the walker she was in her pushchair, I couldn't change her nappy and so she used to cry because she wanted changing. One night she was crying so much, I couldn't stand the noise and managed to push her through to her bedroom so I didn't have to listen to the cries.

It was terrifying and dangerous living there. Not long after we moved in I was on my own and someone was in the garden trying to get into the back door, I rang Daniel and he came back. Whoever was there was gone by the time he'd got there. He ended up putting wood above the fence so it was harder to climb over but I still didn't feel safe.

Another time was when he left me all night; of course I hadn't been able to go to bed and was up. I was in the living room and suddenly there was a big noise from the front door. I was so scared, I looked round the corner and the front door had been kicked in, the bolt broken and the door ajar. What the hell do I do now? Were they coming back? They might hurt me, oh God! I phoned Daniel and told him to get here straight away, he was at that Mandy's with Erin for the night, I found out about a year later that he was having an affair with her but I'll come to that later. So I'm sat there behind the front door scared stiff and then suddenly a young bloke comes to the door and went to push it open. "GET OUT!!!" I screamed. He looked at me shocked and ran, I think he thought the place was empty and had a shock to find me sat there. Daniel came back to find me shaking and the door open and was he bothered, no not really.

There was a third time. Boys were in the back garden trying to get in and I was on my own, I called the police and Daniel but by the time anybody turned up there was no sign of anyone. I was broken into another three times whilst living at that bungalow, once when Daniel and I were over and twice was Daniel himself. Breaking in and nicking the video and a couple of other things to pay for his habit. One of the times he came through Erin's bedroom window, his own daughter's window and at the same time putting a Mother's Day card through the door for me, how low.

The last time we were broken into I managed to finally get a move out of the area because I said to Social Services that I couldn't cope living there anymore. It wasn't safe for Erin and I and if we had stayed I was worried that something serious would eventually happen to us. My carer and I had watched The Exorcist the night before and we were too scared to sleep by ourselves so she got in my bed. A noise work us about 6.30am, Natalie got up and had a look around and put it down to the hamster. Next thing we know, there's a lad wearing a hoodie standing in the bedroom looking over us with Natalie's handbag on his shoulder. She leapt out of bed shouting at him, ran after him but he must have had the kitchen door unlocked already so he could get out quick. We could not believe it, we rang the police and they came out and got a statement. All he managed to take was Natalie's bag, my lighter and my purse I think, but it didn't have anything in it. After that I got moved pretty much straight away but more of that later and back to Christmas.

It was Erin's first Christmas. I don't remember Christmas shopping with Daniel so I've no idea what she had from us. We managed to get down to my Mum and Dads for a couple of nights the weekend before, going down there was so nice, I could be normal for a couple of days and be treated properly. I could go to the toilet when I wanted and a cup of tea and a proper meal cooked for me. Erin opened her presents from Mum and Dad while we were there and instead of watching and helping Erin opening some presents what was Daniel doing? Sleeping, and catching up with all the sleep he'd missed because he never went to bed most nights. Dad filmed it all, Erin opening her presents and her Dad asleep!

I didn't want to go back to that bungalow; I wanted to stay with my Mum and Dad where I was looked after. Christmas Day came, Daniel had to wrap my presents Christmas morning before I got up because he couldn't be bothered to do it at any other time. The fridge wasn't working so we had no food, no Christmas dinner, nothing. We took Erin over to see her other grandparents, Anne and John as they wanted to see her on Christmas day but as soon as we got home Daniel was off out. I was on my own for most of Christmas day, I felt so lonely. I sat and watched the Batman and Robin Only Fools and Horses and tried to watch an old black and white film. The whole day couldn't have been worse, Happy Christmas Grace!

This whole situation had to end soon for my own sanity and health and also Erin's too. Mum and Dad came up for a Sunday; it was probably the only day Daniel stayed in. My Mum was concerned, although she didn't say anything at the time, Erin was wearing a summer dress and it was January, Daniel hadn't done any washing and so this was all she had to wear. I was always nagging him but his mates and his drugs were more important. I remember that day trying to hide a bite mark on the side of my face with my hair so that Mum and Dad didn't notice. We'd had yet another fight and he decided to bite me, I even have a photo with it somewhere. Biting, strangling, slapping, spitting, his hands around my feet threatening to twist my ankles, things thrown at me, it was horrendous! He habit was getting worse. But it was always my fault wasn't it? Why was I nagging him to wash up, do the laundry, take me to the toilet, wash me and leave us all day and all night, couldn't he spend some time with his family? You see we could have had help in but Daniel was too greedy with the drugs, there was no money left to pay anyone else to care and in his defence we didn't have as much money for care as I do now, but if there had been more money he would have spent even more on drugs.

February came and Daniel had this other young lad hanging around with him everywhere he went. I know he was staying at that Mandy's a lot, her and her bloke had split up and so Daniel was there for her like the knight in shining armour he was, to everybody else. One night she wanted dropping off at a club and picking up again and on the way back he popped in with her to show her the bungalow. He would show her a bedroom and it would go quiet, like they were having a kiss or something and then she has the nerve to sit and have a coffee with me. Erin was on my lap and started crying. "I know what she wants" Mandy says. So Daniel took Erin off of me and gave her to Mandy, that hurt me so much. But yeah I found out later on that he was definitely sleeping with her at the time. If you're reading this Mandy, if you can actually read, I hope you're proud of yourself. Leaving a disabled woman on her own all night without her baby while you sleep with her bloke, class!

My electric chair wouldn't work and I had to use my manual wheelchair which I hated. I couldn't stand not being able to get around and be independent. And yes, he would even go out for hours while I was stuck in one position, in front of the TV, but it was okay I had the remote and a phone at hand so what was I complaining for? The electric went one night; Erin was in her walker, I was in my manual chair, no lights, just the street light and the phone handset wouldn't work. I literally had to wiggle and go backwards and forward to try and get my chair from one side of the living room to the other. I needed to get over to the shelf where another phone was, I needed to unplug the phone from the wall and plug the other one in. I knocked over the shelf and managed to do it, how I did I have no idea, I must have some super SMA power from somewhere. I rang Daniel and he was home within half an hour and flicked the electric back on. Don't quote me but I'm sure he wanted to go back out again, I don't think so!

The last straw came when Daniel broke my nose. I have no idea what the argument was about, probably the usual things. I was still in my manual chair as my electric chair still hadn't been fixed and so I couldn't move. We were arguing and he was in my face, suddenly his hand was knocking my face and my nose and head hurt. I looked down and there was blood all over my pink jumper. He just looked at me and said "I think I've broken your nose".

This is all a bit of a daze; I just remember him changing my jumper and putting the blood splattered one in the bin. I don't know if he went straight out or what, I can't remember but I phoned home, told them what had happened and Mum or Dad made that call to Social Services. They had a feeling something was going on but didn't know to what extent and had made calls to Social Services and the hospital before I was attacked for the last time but they were told there was nothing they could do until I asked for the help. Mum says now that I was on the phone to them while he was hitting me at some point just before he broke my nose but I don't remember. Social Services didn't want to do anything at first, they said it was up to me to contact them but I didn't have it in me and things were now desperate.

My eyes were black and blue and my nose was definitely broken, I had physically and mentally had enough and Daniel had too. A lady from Social Services came round the next day and we looked at my options. There was no option, Daniel had to leave as soon as possible and I wanted my baby with me and care in my own home. A couple of care agencies were contacted but they couldn't put the care in for me until after the weekend and it was Friday. So it was decided that Daniel would stay until Monday, which was pretty bad considering what he had done to me, care should have been put in place straight away. Mutual friends of ours, the very few we had left, were going to stay at mine for a couple of weeks and help with my care because the care agency couldn't sort out the 24 hour care that I needed. My situation was rare, nobody had 24 hour care and plus I had a baby to look after. I think Erin went to stay with Anne that weekend and Daniel's friend was staying at mine so I wasn't on my own, Daniel was still about to put me to bed but I was still having to wee myself because he wasn't around still and his mate couldn't take me. Social Services were now involved and I still didn't have the care I needed.

Monday came and I think we had an argument that morning. He smashed Erin's baby bath up and kept banging one of her toys into the wall making dents and I was screaming "GET OUT!" This time he was gone and wouldn't be coming back, only for some of his belongings. It was all over, Erin and I now had a peaceful home. I was advised to phone the Domestic Abuse Helpline by Social Services. I gave them a ring and they basically told me to pack all of his stuff up and not to let him in and I explained that he had left anyway. They advised me to get to the hospital about my nose, get it certified that it was actually broken and press charges but I didn't.

Whether your disabled or not no one should stay in that environment, as soon as a man hits you leave him, don't give him second chances as he'll just do it again and again. Please talk to a friend, don't be embarrassed as it's not your fault.

I never got my nose fixed, it's a sad reminder of what happened whenever I look in the mirror and maybe I should have had it mended. I wish I had done that now and I wish I had pressed charges. If I had done that then maybe Daniel wouldn't of been free to do what he did a year and a half later and I believe what eventually happened to him was Karma, but it was a shame someone innocent had to die.

CHAPTER TEN

Causing a Commotion

Mine and Erin's life was now great. I had two weeks using care agencies giving me time to advertise and employ my own staff, which I've explained about in the chapter about my care.

It was odd going from what I went through with Daniel to having people with me all the time. I would be very thankful if someone made me a cup of tea or a meal. There was someone there all the time to change Erin's nappy or give her a bath. She now had a proper routine during the day and at night. My carers were there for me and for her, what I couldn't do they would do for me. I would try and feed her in her high chair. I could reach, I'm not saying it wasn't messy but it was something I could do. I would read to her and teach her words. Social Services put her into a Nursery as soon as she turned 1, they picked her up in a bus in the morning, dropped her back at lunch time and she loved it. When she was a little bit older she attended the Nursery that was just over the road which was so handy

Anne and John would have Erin for the weekend every fortnight which helped and Daniel would spend time with her there. I was fine with that but wasn't impressed when she came home with her hair cut, her first haircut! Erin had really curly ringlet hair, beautiful it was and still is, but she came back with really short curls. Daniel had got a friend to do it without discussing it with me; Anne said to him that I wouldn't be happy, damn right! Daniel used to pop in and take her out to the park although he did let her down on quite a few occasions.

I still loved Daniel, of course there were still going to be feelings there. I hated him for the way he treated us and for what drugs had done to him but we had a child together and I thought there would always be something there but as I write this I can put my hand on my heart and say there is nothing there now. I hate the bloke, when his Mum died I think anything I felt for him died with her. I met him in town for some reason, can't think for what now and he was with a woman who was friends with that Mandy and seeing him with someone else killed me, it really hurt.

I had a couple of carers who could drive and I used to go down to see Mum and Dad. I was visiting them when Erin took her first steps. She was trying to stay on her feet walking from my Mum to my carer; she kept falling when she was almost there and then started again. She managed it in the end bless her and we all cheered.

Erin was such a happy little girl, full of questions; everything was 'why?' 'What for?' and she was very cheeky, I have no idea where she gets her cheekiness from! She had the odd tantrum but what little person doesn't. I used to tell her to get into the hall; I would shut the door and let her scream and cry until she calmed down. When she was done I would make sure she apologised and she understood what she was apologising for. If she was ever rude or played up for someone I always made her apologise. Everybody always said what a polite little girl she was and still is. I brought her up to have manners and respect people and I have to admit I've done a brilliant job. People always comment on how good and well-mannered she is and how she's a credit to me. I know I can send Erin anywhere and know that she'll always be polite.

Nursery was so good for Erin at an early age; she mixed well with the other children and was popular. There was an incident with the Nursery that I wasn't happy about though. Now Erin is very clumsy, she always has been. She's always falling over; knocking things over, you could never have a Christmas dinner without a wine glass being knocked over. She always had bruises and grazes. The Nursery got in touch and said they were concerned about a couple of bruises she had on her arm and Social Services were informed. I was furious, I tried to explain that Erin was a clumsy, accident prone child but they weren't convinced. They were trying to make out that Erin had been bruised maybe by a carer or somebody at home. They were so concerned they put me, our carer, Erin and social worker in a cab to the hospital. I couldn't believe this; I was in a mood for the whole visit. A doctor had to check her bruises to see if they were done by somebody. The Doctor checked her over and said she was fine. I was so angry, I wouldn't let anyone hurt Erin and nobody ever would while I was around. I said to the social worker why she wasn't sorting real abused kids out! And what made it even worse, the doctor made a comment along the lines of "if you can't look after your own child you shouldn't have had one", how dare she!

My carer and I soon put her in her place, stupid woman. So we were taken back home in a cab and no more was said about it!

Apart from Erin being accident prone, she was a very healthy little girl. She didn't have that many colds or illnesses. The only time she has ever been in hospital, apart from when she was born was when she had a Febrile Convulsion. She wasn't well one afternoon and had a high temperature but she got so hot her little body had a fit. We called an ambulance and they took her to hospital. My carer went with her as I couldn't get in the ambulance and so another carer who could drive took me to the hospital. They got her temperature down and kept her in overnight. It was frustrating because other Mums could stay at the hospital with their poorly children but I couldn't, I mean I could of stayed up all night in my wheelchair, done that before on several occasions haven't I!

We went over to tell Daniel that Erin was in hospital and he came over and stayed for a little while, I stayed as long as I could. I didn't want to leave her but I would be straight back in the morning. When I went to the hospital the next morning, she was running around like her normal self. We got the all clear and took her home. The only other time she was really poorly was when she had Chicken Pox when she was 7. They were all over her body poor little thing; she even has scars now from them. She couldn't stop crying and when you bathed her it was so painful for her, you feel so helpless. And that's been about it, touch wood she stays healthy.

Everything was going great and then something happened that still shocks me now and our lives would be changed, especially Erin's. It was an August afternoon and we were sitting outside with the local radio on when the local news came on. I never really take much notice but for some reason I did this time. It was reported that a 21 year old man had been arrested by police for the murder of a 79 year old lady. We mentioned it and wondered what had happened as you do but never in my wildest dreams would I have thought it was Daniel. I think it was Anne who phoned me and basically said that it was Daniel who had killed that old lady. I was in shock, I think we all were, I know from experience that he's capable of hurting someone but not killing anyone, it didn't make sense.

It was on Central the local news that evening and on the front of the local paper. They showed a photo of this old frail lady and a photo showing the police outside her flat. On the news it was footage from outside interviewing a police officer. The police were saying it was one of the most horrific crimes they had seen. This old lady had disturbed a burglar and the burglar had bludgeoned her to death with a heavy object. It said how everybody was shocked at the murder and how she was always up the shops in her fur coat, how she was the sweetest lady.

Anne rang that evening to admit to me that Daniel was the 21year old arrested and being questioned by the police, the police don't disclose any names until that person has been charged. Nobody could believe it, it was the talk of the local area, lots of rumours flying around and some are so sick I'm not even going to write about it because they weren't actually true.

You see what happened was this; Daniel was doing a lot of burglaries at the time obviously to pay for his drug habit. He was on all kinds of drugs, E's, Acid, Heroin, Coke and I believe he was on Crack Cocaine on the night of the killing and he was injecting too. The injecting started when I was pregnant; I explained why I was having injections every day earlier. Daniel decided he would see what it was like to inject Speed or Wiz as it's also known. There were needles around and he couldn't resist them and that's what started his addiction. It used to break my heart knowing he was in the bathroom doing that, it made me feel sick. When he left, he was living in one of the high rises near mine and I remember him coming over to see Erin and going to the toilet, it was obvious what he was doing in there and I was going mad. Another time he came round with his dodgy druggie mate and asked if he could take a spoon with him, making it obvious they were going to do heroin, both of them excited. The pair of idiots, it makes my skin crawl just thinking about it. And yes, I'm no angel, I admit that but have never done anything like this, this was scary!

Daniel was a proper addict, I think he even tried going to 'Counselling and Drugs Therapy' but he just couldn't kick his habit. I didn't really know much about his life then; he had a few jobs and girlfriends. He turned up with a ginger girl in tow once and he was staying with her a lot. As I said before, he broke into my bungalow a couple of times and also his Mum and Dads and it was the breaking into his Mum and Dads that lead to his arrest.

He'd broken into their house once before and so the second time they had had enough and rung the police. If you're burgled and want to claim on the insurance you have to call the police out so that they can give you a crime number to give to the insurance company. The police went round, took details and that was that or so they thought. Daniel got greedy that night. He went round the corner and broke into the old lady's flat, through the window the same way as he had broken into his Mum and Dads that afternoon. It wasn't late but the lady was already in bed. He stole money from her purse and as he was going through her things she woke up. Daniel was startled and he hit her a fair few times with a tyre lever and ran. Apparently it was a mess, she was a mess, and it's hard to picture anything so horrific. I heard that he went out that night, got out of his face and brought trainers the next day with the stolen money. He got the ginger girl to wash his blood splattered clothes in her washing machine. The lady I think was found the next evening; the police connected the two break-ins and arrested him on the Sunday morning from the ginger girl's flat.

I went round to see Anne and John the day after we knew and had to drive passed the old lady's flat. It was still marked off because it was a crime scene and flowers were outside. Anne was at home with Susan, Susan and I hadn't spoken or seen each other for years so the atmosphere was quite intense, we made small talk but nothing major. Anne was in bits, you can't imagine what a mother would be going through knowing your child was capable of such a crime, but she was always there for him, her baby, and her little boy. His Dad was a different story. Daniel had brought shame to the family and John wanted nothing to do with him. They didn't speak for years, not until John became very ill and they kind of made a truce.

It took three days for Daniel to confess to killing the old lady. They had so much evidence that there was no way he could deny killing her. The ginger girl's flat was searched and the washing machine removed. Daniel's flat was also searched and that was apparently like a drug den with needles lying everywhere. Questioned for three days and going through cold turkey, he was in a bad way, not that anyone should feel sorry for him, far from it. At the end of the day he was Erin's Dad, what the hell was I going to tell her? Thankfully she was only 2 ½ and she didn't see Daniel that much anyway. I was worried for her and for me though, there were rumours going round about wanting him dead because of what he'd done. Were they going to target me because I was his ex and had his child? I remember being quite scared at the time. But the police assured me that we were okay and it was him they wanted not us.

The police convicted him of burglary and murder and he was sent to a jail in Birmingham while he was waiting for trial. The prison that held Fred West before his trial but he ended up hanging himself. The papers named Daniel and it was on the local news. It was really surreal hearing his name read out like that by the newsreader who delivers the news every evening.

Before Daniel was convicted I had a visit from the detective who was in charge of the case, a woman you didn't mess with and she scared the shit out of me. She was interviewing several people to do with Daniel, even his sister. She asked if I could go down to the station and answer some questions, basically they wanted as much shit on him as they could get. I was taken into a small room and it was just me and her. I had to go right back to when I had met him, what our relationship was like before we lived together, the lot. A few things were asked about our sex life that weren't true, Susan had been interviewed before me and had told her things that didn't happen. Susan was always a 'great witness' and told them everything but I was named as the 'hostile witness' because I was careful of what I said. I wasn't going to name drug dealers, I had mine and Erin's safety to think about but it was okay for Susan to say what she wanted. All the police wanted was his abusive history really and I didn't hold back there. The interview was awful, just like the TV and films where they try to twist your words. I was in tears at one point and she asked me what I was crying for, I felt like a criminal myself!

I made the decision that Daniel was still Erin's Dad and that he would still have contact with her, if I had to make that decision now I know it would be a totally different one if I'm honest. I kept the peace for Anne and John's sake, I still wanted them in Erin's life, they were great grandparents and stuck up for me when it was needed which I appreciated. If Daniel hadn't of been in Erin's life I don't think it would have been a massive blow to her, drawing tatty teddy pictures, phone calls and letters doesn't make you a good father. I, with the help of carers, my parents and Anne and John have bought her up all by myself, she's the person she is today because of me not him. Some mothers would have just cut the Dad and the family off in my position and people still wonder to this day why I kept the contact but it was the right decision at the time.

Daniel's sentencing was at Worcester and only took about an hour. I went along with Karen and Daniel's Uncle and Susan was there too. The court room was so surreal it was like you weren't really there and you were watching it on the television. I was sitting on my own by the dock as I couldn't get up to the public gallery. I can't remember much about it now, it seems such a long time ago. The prosecution said their bit, and then Daniel's solicitor said his bit, said how remorseful Daniel was and how he had a drug problem etc. The judge looked at photos of the old lady, apparently you could see them from the public gallery but I couldn't see from where I was and apparently they were really horrific. The judge made his decision and sentenced Daniel to 15 years in prison. He would serve the whole 15 years before parole. As Daniel was taken down I smiled at him.

From day one I took Erin on visits, travelling as far as nearly 2 hours away for some prisons, he seemed to get further and further away. If Daniel asked for a visit I would go if I was able, some prisons he was in weren't wheelchair accessible or were just too far away. I didn't mind going on visits at first, I actually found it quite interesting. The Birmingham prison was the first one, the visiting room was upstairs, a big massive hall. I was searched like everybody else, well as much as they could search me, there was no point doing the metal scan thing as I would set it off anyway. I used to visit there maybe a couple of times a month. One time they asked if I could be transferred onto a prison chair thing, they were told very bluntly 'no'!

Once Daniel was sentenced he was taken a prison in Worcestershire which was a trek, I hated going there. It took so long to get visitors through; it would take a good two hours from signing in at the visitors centre to actually getting into the visit, longer sometimes. He was then transferred to a lifer's prison in Leicestershire which was easier but I used to hate it in the winter driving through the country lanes in the dark and cold. I stopped visiting him for a number of years, I had no car and Daniel was moved to other prisons which was fine by me. Anne still took Erin and once John had cleared the air he went too, so even though I couldn't take Erin she still got to see her Dad. I always tried to protect Erin, I told her that Daddy was at work and that worked out great until John decided to tell her the truth, I have no idea why he told her and wasn't happy at all, if anyone was going to tell Erin the truth about her Dad it was going to be me not him!

There is no love lost between Daniel and I, we were always falling out on the phone, where he's concerned I just cannot bite my tongue and whatever I did or said with the family I felt I wasn't good enough. All I ever wanted was some respect, I was always there for him and his Mum and Dad and I have no bad words to say about them, took Erin on visits, sent him in money at the beginning, went out and got him his clothes. We were always arguing over something, yes there was flirting, but he's a guy in prison and they're all the same. We used to write letters all the time at the beginning and then he would be lucky to get one a year because I couldn't be bothered. We don't speak anymore and I will never be able to sit in the same room as him ever again, I just can't do it anymore and a lot of people say that they don't blame me.

John passed away from Cancer at Christmas 2009 and Anne was diagnosed too which was so sad, both of them together. John had had problems with his back for years and had trouble walking. He was in and out of hospital and took a turn for the worse a couple of months before that Christmas. Anne looked after him at home along with the Macmillan Nurses. We got a call from Anne whilst we were out Christmas shopping, just two days before Christmas to say that he had just passed away. We got over there straight away. John's body was still there in the living room and we stayed with Anne and her Mum until the undertakers came. I didn't want Erin to see John like that but my God she is such a brave girl, it didn't bother her in the slightest. But 14 months later we were in the same situation with Anne.

Anne had lung cancer and had radiation that shrunk the tumour massively but in the September of 2010 she had a fall. She was taken to hospital and was told that she had a tumour in her brain and it was terminal, she only had months to live. It was so sad, but Anne was so lonely without John, they were soul mates. It was heart breaking watching her go downhill so quickly, watching a strong woman ending up like skin and bone. She underwent Chemotherapy, lost her hair and lost so much weight. At this time my Mum was fighting breast cancer (which I'll talk about later) so at the time it was like I was surrounded by cancer. I tried to involve Anne as much as I could, i.e. when I had a psychic night I invited her along and I had her here for her last couple of Christmases. Her last Christmas was sad because she and everybody else knew that it would be her last. She was in a Hospice for a couple of weeks over Christmas and New Year and my Dad picked her up for Christmas Day and bought her to ours and she stayed the night. Both her and my Mum had lost their hair and when they revealed their heads it was like something out of the film Alien Nation, you had to laugh at that! She was very weak and Dad had to help her on and off the sofa and Erin had to help her with the toilet. But she was with Erin and wanted her last Christmas to be with her.

Anne wanted to be at home when she died, she had her sister in law going in to help and Macmillan Nurses going in to her the last couple weeks. I was concerned that she wasn't getting the care she needed, she had a hospital bed down stairs like John and sat in her favourite chair but I just thought she should have somebody going in more or even all the time. I took Erin over as much as I could, she adored Anne, she was the only grandchild they had and both Anne and John loved her to bits. If it was a school night I would take Erin over and she would have tea with Anne. Anne couldn't do a lot for herself at this stage but Erin would put something in the microwave for both of them. The last weekend Erin had with Anne was with a McMillan Nurse too and Anne seemed okay, her 60th birthday was the following week.

I had a call from Daniel the day before Anne's birthday and it didn't sound like it would be long. He had spoken to her on the phone and he asked her if it was soon and she said 'yes'. Of course he wanted to be with her at the end but a lot of arrangements had to be made with the prison, they can't let a prisoner out to see a relative like that unless they really didn't have long to live but Anne went down so quickly there really wasn't time. I phoned Anne at lunch time, she didn't sound good at all, she could just about speak and I told her I would be over later with Erin. When I got there we were told that it wouldn't be long, it was so sad watching her struggle, I just kept thinking 'just let go Anne, stop fighting it now' and as the nurse was asking me if there was any more family that needed to be here Anne slipped away. We all said that John had come to get her so that they could both celebrate her 60th up in heaven; it's a nice way to think of it. I grew closer to Anne once John had died; she reminded me a lot of myself to be honest, strong and never took any shit, both stubborn Piscean women.

Anne left money and the house when she died and it was split between Erin and Daniel, if John had died after Anne everything would have been left to just Erin. Daniel has never supported Erin financially, I have never had a penny from him and so I thought it was time for him to step up, help out a little bit and do something decent for a change. Don't Dad's normally help support their children, I know he couldn't help on a prison wage but he now had some money. But it just ended up in arguments and I was called a 'money grabber'. Maybe I went about it in the wrong way and I hold my hands up to that but when has he ever done anything the right way. He forgets the petrol I used to put in to take Erin on visits or the money I used to send into him on the odd occasion when he was first sent down. I just thought you now have an opportunity to do something nice, make up for the past a little bit, he even talked about paying for a holiday for Erin and I but when it actually came down to parting with some cash he got arsy. I eventually had £5000 off him, yep £5k for 16 years of bringing up his child while he sits on a small fortune. I now had a wedding to pay for with the help of my Mum, yes Erin and I could have had a holiday if he had given me more money as he had first promised but it wasn't enough to do both as I have to pay for a carer too, going on a holiday isn't cheap for me and I now needed the money for my wedding.

15 years later I was offered some sort of counselling through the prison service as it was something to do with him doing a certain course ready for his release. I refused it, a little bit late for that don't you think!

But that's all I will say about Daniel now. I would never have had Erin if it wasn't for him, and she is my world. He is my past now, yes I'm still very bitter about how he treated me and always will be, I'm only human. He is nothing to me now, just Erin's Dad. I've out done any ex partner duties and what I've done for that family has never been fully appreciated, but I've moved on now, it's in the past.

CHAPTER ELEVEN

Hello and Goodbye

Care is the most important thing in a disabled person's life especially when you can't do much for yourself and you need 24 hour care. I couldn't live a normal life without my carers.

My care has stemmed right back from my Mum and Dad to the present day, from 'house mums' at school to 'care staff' at college and then to employing my own PA's in my own home. I've probably got through about 50 carers over the years, I've had some that I've loved and got really close to and there's others that I couldn't stand, didn't want them in my home for one second more. It's all about getting on with someone, a bit like a relationship, if you haven't got that spark then it's not going to work. It's a lot to do with give and take, the understanding that they are here to do a job and for me to be a fair but strict boss. It's taken me years to master it, but I think I've finally got it right. People respect you more if you're upfront and honest with them. I never used to say anything before, just kept my mouth shut and let people walk all over me because I hated confrontation and the fear of being just left in the lurch without anybody, probably because of what I went through with Daniel. But now if something bothers me I nip it in the bud pretty much straight away, well I try to.

I've employed carers through adverts in the paper, young girls ringing up with no enthusiasm thinking it's an easy well paid job, applying because the job centre is on their back to get a job and believe me that seriously doesn't work. I'll ask if they've had any experience in care and they'll say that they've looked after their granny for an afternoon a week or something, not good enough in my eyes. Or some foreign person would ring who couldn't speak much English so that put me off before I even started to explain the job. You have to carry on and be polite, you can't just say 'I'm very sorry, I can't understand you goodbye'. Older ladies would ring and you could hear in their voice that they were older but you can't be ageist, I would always ask their age so I had a rough idea. Even men have rung me which I think is a bit weird, I always state in my advert that I have a young daughter and to me I think it's slightly strange when a guy wants to look after a disabled lady and a little girl and I would always say 'I'm sorry but I'm looking for a woman'.

I leave it for a few days, take people's numbers and if they sound interesting I would ring them back and offer them an interview. I had my questions in front of me, things like,

"What made you apply for the job?"

"Are you okay with personal care?"

"Do you smoke?"…that was always a good one because a smoker would always fidget and say "I'm not a heavy smoker, just one or two a day".

"Can you cook?"

I would ask them about their hobbies and what they liked to do in their spare time just to get some idea of what they were about and if they would fit into my life style. I wanted someone like me, easy going, reliable, who enjoyed a drink now and again, with an uncomplicated family life i.e. didn't have 29 children to sort out and a needy husband. They had to be good with Erin, if they drove then that was a bonus and obviously good with the care. Very hard to find, it's so tricky finding someone that ticks all the boxes and you know as soon as they walk in the door if they're a potential employee or not. Some have walked in and I've instantly thought hmmm you can walk straight back out again, there's no chance!

After I'd interviewed everybody I had to decide who to take on, I wouldn't just take anyone on for the sake of it, there's no way I can live with someone for 24hrs or more if I didn't like them and that would be the same for anybody who spent time in someone's house. I would phone them back and say thanks for coming you but haven't got the job or if they were really unlucky they had, only teasing, it was a bit of a buzz telling someone they had the job. They would normally start within a week or two and I would have them pop in for an hour to talk over their contract, shifts and to show them how to use the hoist, help me with the toilet etc.

But a lot of my carers have been found through other people which I prefer. A friend or someone that works here knows somebody that is interested, I meet them and if I like them then we go from there, sometimes it's better than taking a total stranger on. It's always nerve racking when someone does their first shift, probably more nerve racking for them. I try to make them feel as at home as possible, talk their heads off, watch a bit of TV then go to bed and phew the first shift's done and out of the way.

My first experience of employing properly was when Daniel and I finished. I had agencies in for a month to look after Erin and I. It was okay, I met a lot of nice ladies, some not so nice but I didn't have to see them again anyway. A couple of the carers I knew from college, some young girls that I really got on well with and some I told the agency never to send again. An older lady used to do quite a lot of nights; it was like having my Nan around. She would even bring me things in for the house like tea towels or a plant. But because I had to sit and talk to them it got my confidence back, I wasn't used to being around people, I mean it had just been me, Daniel and his druggy friends for three years.

Because the agency provided my care for a month it gave me the chance to put an advert in the local paper and hold interviews for my own employees. I can remember the phone not stopping; I think I had about sixty calls over about four days. I was knackered and how I wish I had my earpiece for the phone back then, it would have been so much easier. In the advert I had the rates of pay and I didn't state I wanted drivers because I only need a couple at a time. I wanted four carer's to do the weeks shifts between them; it was quite scary because I'd never done anything like this before. I didn't do it all on my own though, I had the help of a council run company. They are there to help you with any aspect of employing, to help you put your advert in, to help you interview, to teach you how to do the PAYE for Tax and National Insurance. It's a lot easier now because I whack it all in the computer, it tells me what I have to deduct. I do the wage slips, pay the Tax every month, job done but back then you had to look it all up on Tax Tables and it got quite complicated. I know exactly what I'm doing now, very organised.

I chose my four, all quite different from each other. One was glamorous and great fun to go out with and drove. One was quite young, a bit of a nutcase in a nice way but she'd worked in a care home for a couple of years and had the experience. One I knew from my college days, she was one of Susan's mates and also drove and we had number four who was very sweet on her interview but a bit of a loon. She was early 20's, married and had a baby but she had the weirdest habits, she would bring her own cutlery in, would have to sleep in my room instead of the living room, and couldn't have gaps in the curtains when they were closed. She couldn't handle me having a poo either, I would have to poo into the bowl underneath the commode then empty it into the toilet, she would hold it at arms length pulling a face making me feel awful, we all shit for God sake! She also brought her 'twiddly' in with her, it was a bit of rag that she used to have to twiddle at night whilst watching TV like a comfort thing, she only lasted about a month.

My carers would come and go as time went on. Some would leave because there would be a huge disagreement between us; I can be quite hot headed sometimes. At times it would be hard to play it by the book, they had contracts and I could be taken to court for wrongful dismissal so I had to be careful, it seemed they had more rights than me. It's not good when you have to pull someone up and then have to be around them till the next day, there's an atmosphere which is the worst thing to have in your home. I've been put to bed when they've been in a mood with me and haven't spoken a word and I don't particularly want to speak to them either, it's quite humiliating.

It's much nicer when somebody comes to you and hands in their notice. They say that they've really enjoyed working with Erin and I but it's time to move on. Sometimes it gets quite nasty, you have to give them the holiday you owe, if any and be civil but you think 'hang on a second this person took the piss out of me and my home, they don't deserve anything' which is quite frustrating.

I've had all sorts of carers with all different stories. I'll give you some examples. I took on this young girl, she answered my advert in the paper, was really lovely on her interview but what a nightmare! Within a few days she was arguing with a boyfriend outside the front of the house. She would go on my computer in my bedroom with the stereo set up in there and the door shut. Her mates would also come round. She took an overdose (not here) and ended up in hospital. £20 notes were going missing out of my purse and Erin's money box and I had a feeling it was her so I made sure I knew exactly what I had in my purse and after one of her shifts the £20 had gone. I phoned her "Don't bother coming back here your sacked!' I said to her.

If someone robs you then I do have the right to sack someone straight away. Within an hour I had her Mum and aunty round saying they were ever so sorry and they couldn't believe she could do such a thing, phew that was the end of her. Well that's what I thought. She stole about £60 in all and I kept it back from the wages I owed her. Her Mum and aunty stopped me in the street and told me if I didn't pay that money back they would take me down 'The Cop Shop' and lots of other threatening stuff. They were common, horrible people and I got scared so had the money outside for them to pick up the next day, it was either that or be threatened more. I wouldn't have given in so easily today I would have said 'come on then!'

I had a carer on Heroin; I had no idea when I took her on that she was a heavy drug user. She looked dirty and rough and would sit in the spare room for ages, then come out with a weird look on her face. She used to have her boyfriend round a lot and the whole situation got weirder. She used to ring me and say "Grace, I'm going to be late into work, I've had my house robbed".

Things just didn't add up, always a drama! I got so down with it, quite scared and I had to call her bluff to get rid of her. I told her that when my Mum and Dad stayed at Christmas they found used foil on the floor, they didn't, but she didn't deny it and that was the end of her.

Another carer acted a bit strange when I had a chest infection once. When she came in to get me up out of bed she had made herself a makeshift mask out of toilet paper so that she wouldn't breathe in my germs. I felt like I had this contagious disease and all I had was a cold!

I've had some complete nutters that have made me laugh so much though. One I had was engaged to get married but when we went clubbing she would literally kiss every bloke she came across. She'd go off and come back 20 minutes later bragging about the blokes she'd just got off with. I couldn't go to the toilet very easily when I was out and had to take with me a bottle for women, the carer would put it between my legs and I would try and aim, well in theory. On a night out with this carer I'd forgotten the bottle so had to grab a pint glass, well trying to catch your wee in a pint glass is a non starter but I think we managed to catch half a pint. Instead of putting it down the toilet she walked out of the toilet, half a pint of wee in hand and put it on the nearest table, we were in stitches! I do apologise to the person who drank my wee by mistake that night, I hear it is meant to be good for you!

There's another funny story about not being able to go. I went out for the night with my brother and friends and there was no disabled toilet in this place and because of the drink I wet myself, I seriously couldn't hold it. There was a trail of wee under me and as I was leaving I skidded and went into a wall, yep skidded on my own wee but I was probably too pissed to care!

Yolandi was one in a million and although she's now back home in South Africa we are and always will be very good friends. I met her at a local pub, I was looking for a new carer who could drive, and I'd had no luck advertising and was worrying about finding someone. It was quiz night and her and her husband were on the table behind us, she'd gone to the toilet and he helped us with the flag question pointing out the South African one. We asked them to join us and we hit it off straight away, it was weird, she was working in a care home but wanted a change, she could drive and she was exactly 10 years younger than me, we shared the same birthday. They came back to mine and I took her on a week later, she stayed with me for three and a half years and only left because she got a teaching job in Thailand. She was a Christian and very opinionated which strained our relationship sometimes. We would have to agree to disagree a lot, and I think we were so alike in some respect that we just clashed sometimes.

Yolandi was a good carer though, she looked after Erin and I really well, and I always remember her husband saying to me on that first night "Yolandi will look after you".

She always said our meeting was fate and God was behind it, we learnt a lot from each other. She was always trying to make me see that God and Jesus existed and I really tried to believe it all, I even went to church with her one Sunday morning, yep me at church, which was the most uncomfortable hour of my life. I appreciate that people have their beliefs but I just couldn't get my head round the whole thing. Yolandi said I had the devil with me that day, maybe I did, I was not into it at all, at least I tried but it just wasn't my thing.

She always had my best interests at heart, always telling me what I should be eating to be healthier, introduced me to herbal remedies and generally wanted to help all the time. She introduced me to new foods, I had never tried couscous before or broccoli. She did great barbecue's, South Africans live for their BBQ's or they're Braai as they called it, they had them every weekend. I loved the way the South Africans got together with their friends and family, ate, and drank every weekend. If I was down she could always cheer me up, sometimes I didn't want to hear her advice but I have to say she was right a lot of the time. Her attitude to other people was very much like mine, we clashed at times but we agreed on a hell of a lot too. She is really missed, we talk now and again on Facebook but it's not the same. She now has a little girl who has slight Cerebral Palsy bless her; it was like she was practising with me getting ready for her own little girl. She came back to England a little while ago for a short stay and I met Dani who was only about 6 months old, very cute she was. When she left for Thailand I knew I would see her again and I did, maybe one day I will again.

I used to let carers bring their kids in, they wouldn't have any child care and I thought well bring them in with you because it was easier than finding someone else to do the shift. It's hard work though especially when they're at the age where they want to grab everything, everything is my level so things are easier for toddlers to reach. I used to think what the hell would happen if we had a fire and they had their kids here, who would they get out first? Your natural instinct is to save your own child so where would that leave Erin? Some of them would just turn up with their kids and I'd think 'please, no not today' but I was too soft back then to say no and sometimes I didn't have much choice. It doesn't happen now, maybe now and again when they're really stuck but no one takes the piss.

I've been left in bed all day before; a carer has meant to come in and not turned up. The carer used to take Erin to school then go home and the next carer would be in at 9am, I used to sleep and sleep if I was not woken. I've woken up and had the feeling no one was here yet, I'd call out and nothing. I'd drop back off to sleep only to wake and still be on my own, panic! I always had my phone by me and back then I could just about manage to phone someone, normally the person that was supposed to be here. They would come up with some pathetic excuse as to why they hadn't turned up. If this happened I would be on my own in bed until the next person went and picked Erin up from school or I managed to find someone to come in, it was so upsetting.

Another example of a carer was Karen. We'd known each for years; she was the girl my brother had as a carer when he moved into his maisonette. She would end up falling out with Ben or me, whoever she was working for, and after a time worm her way back into your life and work for one of us again. We gave that woman chance after chance but she used to mess it up every single time. She was fun, funny and had the same silly sense of humour. She was caring when she wanted to be, sometimes she would come in with little gifts for you. She was a brilliant carer when she wanted to be, but when she had a drink inside her it was a whole different story and you could never trust her with blokes, it didn't matter if it was an ex of yours, a guy you fancied in the pub or friend she would make sure she had them!

She could get most men though, she was tall, blonde, not a bad figure and it just used to upset me, she could never just take a back seat where a bloke was concerned. I think there was just the one time that I beat her with a guy and that was Scott, my brother's carer. I had always had a thing for Scott and she was flirting with him at one of our Christmas do's, back then Ben and I used to have joint staff do's with our carer's. Karen was drunk as always and was trying it on with Scott knowing full well that I liked him but I don't think she got very far. A few months later, I ended up being with him on a couple of occasions, he confessed to me that he had a bit of a thing for me too and had for awhile. It didn't end up going anywhere, he had a girlfriend for years and it wasn't going well and they were on the verge of splitting anyway. I've not seen him since my brother's funeral, I have looked for him but have never found him.

Anyway, back to Karen, the biggest deception was when she started seeing my first boyfriend the guy I saw on and off when I came to college. Tom started coming round; I hadn't seen him for 14 years and a small part of me thought that maybe, just maybe something could happen between us again after all these years. Karen was very flirty with him, but it never crossed my mind that she liked him like that.

I needed another carer and Tom my first boyfriend at college came back into my life and started working for me, there was nothing between us so it kind of worked, for a little while. I had Tom, Karen and my Mum working for me, there must have been someone else but I can't think who it was. Karen started coming round more when she wasn't working, I wouldn't let Tom shower me, so she used to come over and shower me if ever I needed one. They would wait around for one another until one had finished a shift and I didn't think anything of it. We used to have some mad parties and if he was working she would be here and she said to me "I love the weekends here", there was me thinking she really loved being in my company, even in her spare time. They would always be sat on the sofa together and if their legs touched she would say "ooooo Tom stop it".

She would go to bed in the spare room, I would be put to bed and 10 minutes later I would hear her creeping out to join him in the living room, I started to think that something was going on. We would be out, Tom did disco's at pubs and sometimes we went along, his friends would come over and say hi and talk to Karen like they all knew each other, because unknown to me they did.

And then one night I had a call off a mutual friend telling me that Tom and Karen had been seeing each other for about three months, all that sneaking around in my house, I was fuming! No, there wasn't anything going on between Tom and I but that wasn't the point. She denied it; she even had a friend of hers try to convince me that everybody else was lying.

She was due into work the following night; we didn't speak until she had to give me a shower later on. She tried to convince me that he had come on to her, how she didn't want to hurt me, how she loved him, oh please spare me! So what was I meant to do now, be two carer's down and only have my Mum? I had no choice but to just accept that they were now a couple and to just get on with it. What hurt me the most was all the stuff going on behind my back and in my house; I was being let down yet again.

Things just weren't right for months, she hated it when Tom was working here or did anything for me. She would phone my house phone once I was in bed so in the end I had her number blocked. Our relationship was really strained, we'd been mates for years but this really tested us. The rows we used to have were awful, we were as stubborn as each other. Tom always needed to pop somewhere and I knew that he'd be off round hers, he was meant to be here working. The fights the pair would get into and I used to have to listen to both sides, it just got too much and I didn't really want either of them here.

One night in the summer Karen and I went out for a pub meal, had a few drinks and carried on drinking when we got home. It was the final of Big Brother, the year Nadia won, I'd had a bet on her and so I was in a good mood. We rowed that night, she started slagging off my Mum and I can't remember what else it was about, I think things just came to a head. She ended up falling asleep on the sofa steaming and I could not for the life of me wake her up. I yelled at her, I put the stereo up loud; I rang the phones, she didn't budge. She finally woke about 7am in the morning and she put me to bed, I didn't say two words to her, I'd had enough. I didn't have to stay up in my chair anymore that was long gone and there was no way I was putting up with that now. So the next morning Tom was due in, he got me up, I sat in he garden all day and she waited in the spare room until he had finished his shift at 5pm, I didn't say one word to her, it was over between us. I have always said I would never ever speak to that woman again, the next time I saw her was when she cheekily and rudely knocked at my door pissed up wanting Tom at New Year, I told her to 'F' off through the window and I've not seen her since. My care was fine; I had somebody else who wanted her job so I didn't lose out.

As for Tom, he stayed with me for another five months, I ended up sacking him because he just used to take the piss and the final straw was when he came in pissed one evening and then said he needed to go back out because his son needed him. "No, if you walk out that door then you have no job", I said. He went, but what a relief, he was just dragging me down, but yet again I was okay for care, there's always somebody there to fill the gap, luckily.

But the Tom saga didn't end there. Some years later we started talking again and he was so sorry for what he had done to me and I was willing to give him one more chance. Karen and Tom lasted two years, I don't really know the ins and outs and I don't really care but he didn't see her anymore. I needed another carer, somebody who could drive, Yolandi was leaving for Thailand and Tom said he could do any shift, he would never take the piss out of me again and we were getting on better than ever and so like an idiot I took him back on but for only one night a week. It really worked out, it was so nice having a guy around instead of women all the time, we had a laugh and the pair of us had brilliant banter. I would get him to drop Erin and me off into town or at the cinema; it was great having that freedom. But he started taking the piss again, would help himself to food, my tablets were going missing, he would leave the house work and sometimes wouldn't be up to take Erin to school.

I was having new flooring and I sent Tom down to the shop to pay for my floor with my credit card. Didn't think anything about it, two weeks later I received my statement and he had taken out two lots of money totalling £450 from cash machines. I called the police and had him arrested and he was there on the CCTV camera's withdrawing the money. It went to court, I didn't need to go because he had no choice but to confess, he got a 1 year suspended prison sentence, 200 hours community service and had to pay the courts the £450 back and the courts paid me £50 a month. It wasn't so much about the money, as I will get that back but it was about the trust, I'd known that guy for 22 years, how could he of done that to me. People said it was wrong robbing a disabled lady he worked for, yes, but firstly it was someone he'd known for a very long time. Yes, I was stupid taking him back on but I was desperate for a driver and thought maybe he had changed, but I was very wrong. I had a massive problem trusting people anyway but this has made me even worse. I will never have anything to do with the guy again, good riddance!

At this present time I have four carer's. Maria is back with me, she took over most of Yolandi's shifts; we went through so much over the Richard (my future boyfriend -more about him later) business it's nice to have someone that really understands what went on back then and doesn't judge me. Saj has been on and off working for me for nearly 10 years. She had a year out working at other places but hated it, she was also on maternity leave but is now back full time with me and says it's the best job she's ever had. She's like my little sister and I love her and Maria to bits. My Mum retired, she had worked for me for 9 years and now we get on better than ever. She looked after me well, did the horrible jobs like cut my toe nails and when you're ill who do you want to be with, yep your Mum, and it worked. Sometimes it was hard drawing the line between Mum and carer or Nanny and carer but we didn't have too many problems.

My care is easy; it's the same thing everyday. I don't even have to ask much now, if I look uncomfortable in bed they can see and will move me without me having to say because they know. I'm hoisted all the time. I do wish I could just jump in the shower though as I have to transfer on to a shower chair in my sling so the slings wet. Then after, hang in the air dripping into a bowl underneath me before I can get onto the bed to dry and put a new dry sling in.

I have my car that my carers and James, my husband drive. Before you could only have two people on your insurance but now I have an open insurance so anybody with a driving licence can drive it. I tend to do the shopping with Erin, we love having a good look round the shops and always buy more than we need, as girls do.

I have Annabel and Jules, Annabel went to school with Maria and has known her for years and Jules is Annabel's friend. I've had the same four, apart from my Mum leaving, for nearly four years now, it's all running well. I have to pull them up on the house work sometimes but that's nothing to what I used to have to put up with. I know I can rely on them and they won't let me down. Social workers always compliment me on how well I run things, a lot of people have trouble with their care and as you've read I've had no end of trouble but I deserve that good care, I've worked hard for it.

CHAPTER TWELVE

Girl Gone Wild

Some people would think fair play and that I must have some bottle and some people would think I was just mad. I've met thirty one men through the internet over eleven years, most of them off social networking sites and some I've got to know through chat rooms or AOL messaging, well back in the day it was that. I met a lot of guys through Face Party and now Facebook. It's not a seedy thing if you're sensible and know what you're doing and I have to say I was a pro!

I always wondered 'what if my man is a guy online' you never know. They would see my profile; in my photos I looked good. Not being big headed but I did look good, the only thing was I never showed my wheelchair, I cropped it out. I always thought if they saw that I was disabled and in a wheelchair they wouldn't want to get to know me. I know honesty is the best policy but I wouldn't have met half the men I had if I hadn't cropped my photos. And yes I know, they're not worth it if they didn't want to know, but I just wanted to be given the chance before they made up their mind about me.

So I would chat to them, exchange photos and speak to them on the phone and they would still not know that I was in a wheelchair. I sounded normal and I was always told I had a sexy voice which added to the mystery about me. They would always ask me questions about myself and I always seemed to be able to bend the truth slightly. I would start feeling guilty and knew they needed to know the truth, if I was going to meet them then they definitely needed to know.

I always seemed to pick the right moment to tell them though, for days I would be dreading it and worried they wouldn't want to know me anymore but I would just think if they are like that then who cares, their loss, but if I really liked them I would be secretly gutted.

Normally I would tell them in chat conversation "Look there's something I have to tell you" I would say. I would explain that I'm in a wheelchair and basically have weak muscles. I would try and explain to them that I was just a normal woman who had a disability, but it was always very hard explaining the ins and outs.

Once I had told them there would be a pause and I would be sat thinking 'oh God, what are they going to write back? ', it would be the longest pause. Every single one of them would say back "it's fine, it doesn't bother me, I like you for you and yeah it is a bit of a shock." It was such a big relief when they knew.

But the biggest test was if they carried on talking to you, most of them did and still wanted to meet up and some would erase you off their msn or not bother to contact you again but that happened very rarely. Thirty one dates later and I must of being doing something right!

My first dabble with the internet was at my brother Ben's house, he'd just got AOL and he showed me what you could do on there and how you could chat, well at the time it was amazing! A little box came up on the screen known as an IM, your Instant Messenger and you would type to this person. Well that was it I wanted it, to be able to chat to someone in another part of the country or even the world was unreal and very exciting.

I started chatting to this guy who was I think from the south of England. I met him in a chat room and we chatted all night for hours, I was in love! Funny to think back now but it's so easy to fall for a personality just like that, this guy didn't even have a photo but I was smitten. I couldn't wait to get back online to chat to him again, this was before texting so it was either chat on the phone or meet online. I would ask my brother if I could go round and use the internet, I couldn't very often as back then BT charged your internet use by the minute and it soon added up and also Ben wanted to use it to chat to some girl from the states that he had fallen for.

I chatted to this guy when I could and we even spoke on the phone. I found out he was married and had kids, not a good start but funnily enough it's where it ended too. We didn't speak much after that, just lost contact and it was hard as I couldn't get to use Ben's internet that often. So I decided I'd get my own computer, just a second hand one out of the paper would just do me for now, all I wanted it for was to chat and surf a little.

My first computer did the job but was so slow, I couldn't surf as the pages would take so long to open, but I could get e-mail and chat. I would chat for hours running up huge phone bills, but there wasn't a lot else in my life apart from Erin and it was such a buzz getting attention from guys who thought you were beautiful and funny and you made their day just by sending them a witty e-mail. I've always been a big flirt and I would have guys eating out my hand, they found me sexy and I loved the attention.

I will tell you about my dates as they are quite funny, I've met some right characters, some nice, some very good looking, some not so nice looking and some that were damn right weird. Some I've seen again, some are friends for life, some I would never want to see if they were the last guy on earth and one was my partner for three years so I haven't done too badly.

My very first date was a disaster. I met him at a pub outside of Coventry because I think he was from the outskirts of Birmingham. My carer and her boyfriend came with me, there was no way I was going on my own, you didn't know who you were meeting and me being so vulnerable I never wanted to chance anything. We had a drink, the pub was heaving, I never like places that are busy so I felt uncomfortable from the off. Mr S really couldn't get his head around me and was rude, I didn't like him at all but it didn't put me off.

A few weeks later I met Mr P, he came round to the house, he didn't live too far away, and someone was always with me so I was pretty safe. We got on great, a bit wet for my liking but the next day he e-mailed me to say that he had just been diagnosed with a tumour, bit weird, on a Sunday and just like that hmmmm I don't think so. I never saw him again.

Mr N was the strangest one of all. He was from Wales and was meant to be staying for the weekend 'eeeekkk', he had to travel to Coventry on the train and be picked up from the station. On the internet his screen name was Vandamme, he had no photo and my God wasn't I in for a shock! Vandamme was more like Les Dawson, no offence to Les Dawson but I was expecting someone totally different. In came this short, fat, hairy man and my heart just sank, he was the most vulgar man I think I've ever met and bugger, he was here for two days, how on earth was I going to cope? So I got drunk and oh no I ended up kissing him, I don't know what possessed me, I think my beer goggles were running over time that night. He stayed in my bed but nothing happened, thankfully!

Whilst I was entertaining in the living room Karen and her mate went through his bag. They found a lot of medication, anti depressant this, anti depressant that and sleepers, which they stole, I didn't agree with that but he was so odd I really didn't care, they even hung his dirty underpants from the light shade!

The next day a load of us went for a meal and he was so rude, loud and his language was disgusting, I didn't know where to put my face and we had kids with us. In the end we told him to go back home to Wales, none of us could put up with him anymore. He cried like a baby and off he went, phew! The next night I had an IM from one of his friends saying he had taken an overdose. This internet dating was beginning to be a bit of a nightmare or maybe it was the guys I was meeting, I was getting slightly put off by it.

Mr M was next, I met him in town. We got on great, nothing happened romantically between us though I think he wanted it to but I didn't like him like that, such a lovely guy though.

Mr G lied about his age, told me he was 10 years older than he was, why lie?!

Another Mr M this one from South Africa, we met in town again and he was the first guy I actually fancied, he was a business man and I'd only started chatting to him the night before. He said meet me tomorrow and I thought oh what the hell and agreed. We had a drink and he said he liked me, had to go off back to his factory and he would come over to mine, I thought my luck was in. At home I waited and waited but he didn't turn up, later he rang me to say sorry he couldn't make it because his factory had been broken into whilst he was with me and he'd be in touch. The next day I received an e-mail from him, basically he accused me of having something to do with his factory being broken into. Couldn't believe what I was reading, I told him he was off his trolley and not to bother me again!

Then there was Mr D and Mr G. Mr D was married and was also seeing another woman, he owned a hotel and we would always chat late at night. He came round one evening for a few hours, we liked each other but it wouldn't have gone anywhere. Mr G came up with his mate on New Years Eve, he was a scouser and I love that accent. I slept with him, well we didn't have sex but we did other things and the next day it was really awkward, he would hardly speak to me then he'd be on the phone talking to a girl. We kept in touch for a bit, he told me he'd met someone and that was the end of that.

So that was my first year of internet dating, not a good start so I stopped for awhile.

After a break I started chatting to Mr A from London, he was so sweet to me but yet again no photo, why hadn't I learnt my lesson? He had a photo but he must have been a teenager when it was taken, he even said he'd done modelling. He wanted to meet and I put it off because of the lack of photos and I eventually gave in. He came up on the train and my carer's boyfriend went to pick him up, he'd chatted to him on the phone and on the internet too so he was excited about meeting him.

Mr A had a disability, I think he told me he had a bit of a limp but I wasn't fazed by that, I mean how could I have a problem with that?! What really annoys me is when they've not honest, I've met a couple like that, I try to explain as much as I can about me but when I meet a guy that is properly disabled well then that pisses me off. As soon as he came in the door I didn't like him, not because he had a disability, he just wasn't my type. I made that pretty clear; I have one of those faces where if I don't like you then you know about it. I said to him that we'll just be friends and he took a bit of a funny one with me. He stayed the night and the next morning I was violently sick and wasn't well at all, could hardly speak to him the next day and he went home back to London and I never spoke to him again.

Then there was Mr T who isn't really worth mentioning only that our song was 'When You're Gone' by Mel C and Bryan Adams and he sent me a copy which was quite sweet.

Then Richard came into my life, I'd been chatting to Richard for awhile now, he was in Coventry, single, lived with his Mum, 4 years older than me, worked, no children and was always there to chat to if I ever needed someone to talk to. He was becoming a really good friend to me, not great looking, even in my situation I admit I can even be slightly shallow at times, but he was the sweetest guy. He wanted to meet up and I kept saying no and in the end I said "Ok, but I'm only meeting you as a mate though".

We met at a nightclub and he was really quiet, you could tell he wasn't used to clubs and he was only drinking coke. He sat staring at me, he couldn't take his eyes off me bless him and we sat together not saying much but, well you can't in those places because you can't hear. Somebody knocked a coke into his lap and after awhile he wanted to go home, bless him.

We carried on chatting online and this time it just felt different, we met again at the same club and he chatted a lot more, he was a shy person anyway so fair play to him!

In the summer I moved house and it wasn't far from Richard, within walking distance from him. He came to my house warming and hardly said a word to anyone and that was the first time he met the family and then it was New Years Eve which was the turn of the century and the new chapter in my life. We'd been out over to our local and came home before midnight, Richard had been into town to see the fireworks and thought he'd pop into mine on the way home. We flirted and I thought do you know what he's nice, he's growing on me, I never for once thought things would end the way they ended with him, looking back now I still find it hard to get my head around it.

Richard was now in my life for the next three years so no more internet dating. I thought I'd finally found the guy for me, someone that would finally put up with me. It wasn't all perfect, but on the whole it went quite smoothly and most importantly I was looked after and treated like I should have been treated. He even gave up work to look after me as a carer (the smackhead) was taking the piss and he hated seeing me so upset all the time. It worked for three years, he looked after me brilliantly!

Richard passed away after three years of us being together and thought I would never get over it but I'll explain what happened in the next chapter. I needed to move on, drinking wine heavily every night wasn't doing me any good. I would open a bottle or a box about 5pm and drink it until bedtime when I'd be very drunk. At weekends I would be up all night chatting on the internet, I guess I just needed the company.

I was still really into the Reality TV Yahoo group and started flirting with a guy on there. We started texting and spoke on the phone and he said he'd come up to Coventry; he'd have to stay the night. We met at the local for a drink, got on well though he wasn't my type at all. He would come up every four months or so and we became really good friends. We never had sex because he was on the larger side so physically it would never have worked. This went on for about two years, until I found out that he had come on to one of my carers. I don't care who you are but if you're a guest in someone's house you don't start coming onto my mate especially when I'm in bed. I'm not able to get up and see what's going on and he took advantage of that; he was meant to be my friend. I never wanted to see him again and the feeling was mutual.

A couple of months after Richard died I started chatting to this guy called Jim. We would be up talking all night, he was someone I could confide in and he would always be there for me; and he was cute. I wanted to speak to him on the phone but he kept making excuses, it turned out he was deaf. I didn't care, I felt closer to him because he had a disability too and he was honest. He lived in Bolton, not around the corner but we managed to meet up and he came down to Coventry one night, well it ended up about 4 in the morning by the time he'd got here. We got on great; it was difficult for me because of him being deaf. He had hearing aids but still couldn't really hear much and if you weren't looking at him then he wouldn't have a clue you were talking to him. But he was such a nice guy and we were really silly together. We went to bed about 7 in the morning, he slept in my bed and I told him nothing was going to happen, well that's what I told him. So I'm lying on my side in bed facing the wall and he lies behind me, his hands start wandering and then he's trying to go a little bit further, further than I wanted. He tried to find a certain area, and finds it and I'm telling him to stop, "Jim, stop it. No!" he can't bloody hear me can he!

I can't move and he can't hear; what a great pair we made! I'm wriggling and making all the signs to stop and he finally realises that I'm protesting; stops and says sorry. We still laugh about it now; we call it 'The night of the wrong hole'.

We stayed in contact and we both liked each other but Bolton was just too far away, he would always say he was coming down but would text or e-mail me last minute to say he couldn't make it, but that was Jim, lovely guy but would always let me down. We did go to Blackpool for a weekend though, my carer and her boyfriend, Jim and I. Blackpool wasn't far from Bolton. We had to go and get him on the Friday night, drop him back on the Saturday and then he managed to get there and stay with me on the Saturday night, we had such a good weekend. I went to see a Clairvoyant on the front and she told me that the guy I was with was my soul mate and I would be with him forever, yeah right and she charged me £50! Nothing came of me and Jim but we're still mates now.

And then there was the guy in the personals from the local paper. It was a drunken night; we were looking through and decided to listen to a few ads. They would leave a message about what they were looking for and if you liked the sound of them then you could leave them a message and I think I liked the sound of a couple and left a voice message. A couple of days later we were out having a family meal and my phone rings, it's one of the guys I left a message for saying how he liked my message and I sounded lovely. We carried on texting and we started chatting on the phone. He sounded nice enough; a bit too full of himself but I thought I'd give it a go and meet him, what did I have to lose. Again I met him at a pub not far away and in he walked with a massive bunch of flowers which were lovely, a really nice thought. He was in a nice suit, had lovely teeth, but had a bit of a Delboy thing going on. He had a sovereign ring on nearly every finger and I hate them, might be safe to say that I have a bit of a phobia of them! As the wine flowed we got on better, we were chalk and cheese and at times we clashed but I had fun. He even got me to go to a Greek Restaurant, I thought he was treating me until it came to the bill and he didn't have enough for the two of us. He got quite naughty as we ate, what he was showing me wasn't very appealing while you eat believe me; thank God the restaurant was empty! He came back to mine and stayed the night. My Mum was due into work the next morning, "Who the hell was that?" Mum asked.

He sent me a couple of texts after, even one saying how lovely and genuine I was and if I ever needed anything then I was to ring him, I never did.

Now Mr P was nice, I met him through Yahoo. I think I messaged him and he replied. Gorgeous, blonde, cheeky looking, just my type, I have a thing for fair haired guys. We e-mailed and chatted, spoke a couple of times on the phone and it turned out he was married, damn. I really didn't care which was wrong I know and the weird thing was he lived just over the road; we only had to cross one street. So we used to go backwards and forwards when his wife was asleep or out. I know it was wrong, I'm not proud of myself and I can see it from the other side now that I'm married myself. I really liked him and we just clicked but nothing was ever going to become of it. He was only after one thing which he never got. I wanted more from a man than that. He ended up being my Gardener; until he started being unreliable and I got engaged.

I met a few more guys but nothing to really write about. Then I met an Asian guy from Birmingham. The first date went great but the second not so, basically he just wanted to have sex with me and I wasn't having any of it! He pestered me all night and when he finally realised I didn't want to he went home in a mood and I never heard from him again, thank God I said no!

A couple more guys, a Turkish guy who was big and strong who wanted to take me shopping and I could have anything I wanted, I didn't take him up on his offer and a guy who worked in a wholesale store, just friends but when ever my carer walked out of the room he would come over and try it on with me but I kept telling him to stop!

And there was the guy that came around at about 1 in the morning, I was quite drunk and the situation was 'I don't like you but I like your carer'! That used to drive me mad. It just makes you feel inadequate, I have to have a carer there and it's not nice when a guy says how great they are and not you. I make all the effort to look nice, to have my hair done, to tan etc and they prefer your carer who's not made an effort because it's not their date. It's not how you look though, it goes deeper than that, most guys just can't handle a woman in a wheelchair and I take my hat off to any able bodied person who finds love with someone in a wheelchair as it's not the easiest thing, you can either cope with it or you can't and I seem to come across men that just can't.

Mr M was nice, we'd been chatting online for a while and we decided it was time to meet. We chatted all night and when he came to go he tried to kiss me but I went really shy. I didn't really hear from him again either although it was probably the text he got the next morning about him that wasn't meant to be for him. A friend asked me how it went and I replied that "He was ok, nice enough" and oh shit, I sent it to him by mistake. As soon as I sent the text I realised what I had done but it was too late! You don't want to hear that you're just 'nice enough' do you?!

It really does sound like all I did back then was meet guys, it wasn't as sinister as it sounds, I would get chatting to them and we would just decide it would be nice to go for a drink. Some of them I'd really fancied and I would really hope there was something between us and others it was pure friendship. I used to get so nervous and every single time I would just think to myself 'why am I putting myself through this yet again?', but it always seemed like the next thing to do once you've been chatting to someone for awhile.

Then there was the guy from South Africa, I had Yolandi working for me that night and so there was a lot of conversation. He was quite cute but he was a little strange. We sat outside at the local and he hated smoking and if anybody around us lit up he would make us move. He rang me a couple of times and he knocked the door once but I had no make up on and pretended I was out.

I was also talking to this guy from Stourbridge, he was lovely and we just clicked straight away. He was into Hypnotism and he wanted to be an actual Hypnotist. We would talk about it a lot. He said that he'd been hypnotised before and all anyone needed to say was these 3 words and he'd go under until you said 'wake'. He told me these 3 words, I won't say them because if he ever did read this he would be hypnotised, well that's what he used to make out or I was just very gullible. He would call me 'Goddess' yeah I know, funny! I used to ring him in bed and say these words and he would just change, his voice would change. He used to get off on it and get rude on the phone. I used to type the 3 words when we were chatting or in a text and I would once again be his 'goddess' until I said 'wake'. He told me that he'd do anything under my command so I told him to send me flowers but did those flowers arrive, no! Maybe he was just winding me up but it was all a bit strange. We were going to meet but he kept backing out and we just stopped speaking. Actually, 'MIND BLANK BLACK' .... Your Goddess is here!

At the end of 2007 I met Mr A. So lovely, a really nice family man but there wasn't the spark we both hoped for. Although we did see each other a couple of times after and had a cheeky kiss. We're still in touch through Facebook.

That was all for a year, I didn't meet anyone. I started chatting to a guy from Facebook at the end of 2008 who fascinated me! He worked at a funeral directors and did all the embalming etc. We just said hi on passing and started chatting online properly and then one night he gave me his number. He and his job really interested me, we would text all the time and my heart would do somersaults when a text came through from him, I was really falling for this guy and he said the feeling was mutual. I couldn't stop thinking about him, there was just something between us and he even said he was falling in love with me. I couldn't wait to meet this guy and I wanted it all to go so perfectly. Maybe this was the guy who would cope with my disability, I mean he must be a pretty strong guy to be able to do the job he does and I respected him so much. We met after a month of heavy flirting and chatting. He came over and I thought he was lovely but I drank some strong duty free vodka and he was sober as he was driving and I don't think he could handle me. He ignored me the next day, came up with that old excuse of 'oh I lost my phone' hmmmm. We messaged a few times but he backed off and it was obvious he wasn't interested. I wasn't the woman he thought I was and to be honest it really upset me. I really liked him but it wasn't the same for him.

The last guy I met was so lovely. We used to chat late at night and at first he annoyed me because he would just want to be rude on his webcam and I'm not really into that, to be honest it puts me off a guy. He always popped up (literally) at the weekends and he was always asking me out for a drink but I always said no. He was married and had three kids so it wasn't the most ideal situation. I told him about my disability and he wasn't bothered, damn that wasn't going to get rid of him either! We didn't talk for awhile as I didn't go on and chat as much. And after about a year we started chatting again but this time he was different, he just seemed far nicer and we would chat for ages, it was like he grew up! He told me that he'd split from his wife and he was still interested in me so when he gave me his number I thought there wasn't any harm in it. Our texts were funny, he loved his music like me and we were always texting lyrics of songs to each other, he made me laugh! We would talk on the phone for hours, we were just silly, and I felt I could finally just be myself.

Thing is though, he hadn't split up from his wife; but by then it was too late, I was really fond of him and he was a big part of my life for about six months. He worked nights in a home for people with dementia which was great for us as we could talk at night on his breaks or we could text without 'the mrs' finding out. Then in the day he would be on the phone to me when he woke up because 'the mrs' was at work. We arranged that he would come and stay the night and he told his wife he was staying the night at his brothers.

We got on brilliantly, I felt so comfortable with him! We had such a nice evening, even in bed he made me laugh. He would even turn me and get me comfortable, it just seemed natural to him. We tried to have sex but I think we had difficulty because he had to learn how to do it without hurting me but I fully trusted him. It was one of those nights you didn't want to end, he kept telling me how lovely I was and I was happy! The next day he text to say what a great night he had, which was a huge relief. The next night he stayed with me he told his wife that he was working. "But won't she know you've not worked when she looks at your pay packet?" I use to ask "won't she see that you've been on the phone for hours when your phone bill comes in?" but he always insisted she wouldn't find out.

You see, Mr T was Indian and it was an arranged marriage, he loved her but he wasn't 'in-love' with her, well that's what he told me. With me I was the escape he wanted and needed. She did find out about our first night though, not that he was with me but that he wasn't where he said he was and she questioned him. Another night he went into work and they told him he shouldn't have been in, he didn't want to go home so he asked to come to mine instead. I hadn't done my hair and had hardly any make up on, so hairspray and some eyeliner later I said yeah why not.

What we had was great, it suited me and it suited him. We got on really well and I fancied the pants off him. I knew his situation and didn't ask for more than he was able to give but it all had to end didn't it, I was happy wasn't I so of cause it was going to end somehow.

I hadn't heard from him for a little while and he phoned to say that his wife knew about us and he had to keep his head down for awhile. Apparently another woman who he'd seen before rang him while he was at home, his phone was in his coat pocket and his wife answered it, she asked if he was there and his wife had a go at her and told her it was his wife and to not phone again. See, I knew the rules, I would never phone him when he was at home unless he told me it was ok to and I never had his house number, he always rang me on withheld. So his wife decided to go through his phone, he used to save a lot of my texts and she read through them and asked who Grace was. Rumbled, big time, I was gutted. Because they were Indian it was a huge family thing resulting in him staying at his Dads for awhile until the whole family got together to 'decide what to do'. He rang me a couple of times to tell me what was going on but basically he couldn't do anything for a long time, he was too scared to do anything anyway. I was even worried that they would knock on my door but they didn't have a clue who I was and he would never have let them hurt me anyway.

That was it, he phoned me a couple of months later to see if I was ok and he even said then that he would be in touch when everything had died down but he didn't, he was probably way too scared. I missed him; I loved the fact that I could just be myself with him. And that was the last man I met off the internet, I just didn't have it in me to meet anyone else, I really couldn't be doing with being let down yet again.

And that was it for a couple of years, I guess I kind of gave up, really didn't have it in me to meet anyone. And a friend suggested I should go on a dating website for disabled people. I wasn't sure about this but she said maybe start trying to find somebody from the other angle, put it out there that you are disabled first, maybe there were carers on there who would love a disabled lady like me. So I signed up to a few, only thing is you have to pay for them and they're expensive and I wasn't prepared to pay. When you joined you had free messages but once they had ran out you couldn't read them unless you paid. There were some 'normal' guys on there but like a lot of 'normal' sites there was no one that stood out, haha, see what I did there!

There was this one guy that messaged me, said he was in the army and sounded quite genuine. We chatted and even spoke on the phone, he seemed nice apart from wanting photos of me and 'the chair,' so I sent him one and he wanted more. We added each other on Facebook but he only had about twelve friends and guess what, yes they were all women in wheelchairs. I ended up deleting him and we never spoke again, I think he may have had a bit of a fetish. So that put me off, that and having to pay to message someone.

I'd been using a site off of a Facebook site called Social Central. Basically you tagged someone's photo and you could send them a message, I'd got talking to quite a few men this way, it was free and easy to use. A guy from Bristol tagged me quite a lot and basically asked me out, and I made up some excuse and said no. Awhile later he asked me again and I told him the truth. His response was lovely, he said it was an honour to know me and he really didn't have a problem with it so we spoke on the phone and he seemed lovely, well he was lovely, but had issues. We arranged that he come up for a night when Erin was at my Mums for a few days. The night went well, he was great with me and nothing fazed him, even the hoist didn't bother him, I normally hide it until I need it.

"You are everything and more", he told me. That was the nicest thing someone had said to me in ages. When he left to go home on the Sunday he said 'love you' which really threw me, it was too early to be saying stuff like that. I liked him, wasn't that blown away but I thought maybe he could grow on me.

We were texting and he kept thanking me for a lovely night, we spoke on the phone that night and everything was good. It was another 6 weeks until I saw him again, Erin went to the Dominican Republic with Mum and her Husband so we made plans for him to come up and stay. The plan was for him to come up for about four days but in the end he stayed for six, big mistake. It was his birthday on the Saturday and I was flattered that he wanted to spend his birthday with me, so I went all out. I wanted to spoil him and make a fuss because that's what I'm like; I bought balloons, banners, a few presents, all presents with thought put into them and even a cake! Why did I bother, I'm not sure if it was appreciated or not, although he did say thank you. I just found the whole situation weird. I really made an effort, got lots of shopping in, take away ordered, went over to the pub for dinner, took him with us to the X Factor auditions in Birmingham, McDonald's on the way home and did he ever put his hand in his pocket, no!

Nothing happened between us in bed either, he would lie behind me and have his arm around me but that was as far as it went. He never made himself a coffee, offered to wash up, never thanked anybody for his meals and said it was nice. I got angrier and angrier, it showed in my skin, if I'm stressed or ill then my face breaks out in dry irritable sores, I have no control over it, Saj kept saying to me "Calm down Grace, your skins getting worse", my skin flares up red and dry when I'm stressed, but I couldn't help it.

I was ill though on the Monday, caught a cold so wasn't myself and he was off work anyway because of a bad shoulder but still this was no way to impress a girl that you're meant to be keen on. So on the last night I said to him there was no future in us, he was upset and apparently I hurt him but I'm not that desperate for a guy that I'm going to put up with that. And if the guy is reading this, I made every attempt to make your week nice, rude!

I've even been told since by a couple of guys I've met in the past that I'm lovely and they actually really fancied me. I'd say about 85% of my dates have gone well so I should be pleased with that. But now I'm married and the only dates I have now are with my husband.

Oh and before I forget .... and WAKE!

Chapter Thirteen

Don't Tell Me

Richard (the guy I had met online and met in the club) and I had been together for almost three years now. Our life was settled, Erin was doing well at school and we were a lovely little family with no worries and things were going well for us. Our lives were soon turned upside down forever all in one day.

Monday 25th November 2002 started like no other. Richard woke Erin up for school at 7.30am, she got dressed, he did her breakfast, I was in bed and they were just about to leave the house like normal when there was a knock at the door. I could hear a man's voice but didn't recognise it and thought 'oh maybe it's a parcel from Ebay or something'. Whoever it was came in and I had a feeling something was wrong, something didn't feel right.

I shouted out to Richard and asked what was going on and he came in and said it was the Police, 'THE POLICE?!' What the hell did they want??! I had had no dealings with the police since all that business with Daniel, oh and once when Erin rang 999 by mistake. They came round to see if everything was ok, told Erin she wasn't to ring 999 again and she thought she was going to end up in prison like her Dad was, bless her. I think a female police officer came into the bedroom and asked if I could get up and I explained that I couldn't move without anybody's help and needed Richard. What she was about to tell me I just couldn't get my head round. Richard was being arrested for Child Porn. No way, not Richard, the nicest, sweetest man you could ever meet being accused of being a monster, they've got it wrong surely, it's a big mistake!

Richard had to get me up and dressed and I had a female Police Officer stand at the door which was degrading, I was also on my period which made it worse. They had to have a police officer in the room just in case anybody tampered with the computer or did anything else. As Richard was getting me up I said to him "What the hell have you done?" and I also said "Swear on my life you're telling the truth?" all he kept saying was. "I haven't done anything", he kept insisting.

As soon as I was presentable I went into the hall where two police officers and an inspector were waiting for me. The female PO was in the living room keeping Erin amused. I asked what was going on and they told me that Richard was being arrested for downloading child pornography and it was to do with Operation Ore, an operation to crack down on child pornography around the country. Apparently Richard had used his credit card to access a child porn site on the internet. I was still gob smacked. "But Richard is no Gary Glitter." I innocently said to the officer.

Gary Glitter had just been convicted of child porn and Richard and I used to say how sick that was, I didn't have a clue about any of this only what I read in the papers. They said he was being arrested and they needed to take him down to the police station to be questioned. They told him that they would have to handcuff him, and then led him outside to the police car. Watching those cuffs going on his wrists was heartbreaking. It was embarrassing; I don't think many people were about outside but still. I seriously didn't think I was ever going to see him again, that day was the longest and hardest day of my life.

Once they had taken Richard away they sat with me in the kitchen and tried to explain more to me, I still didn't believe what was going on. I rang Maria, asked her if she could come in and I'd explain to her what was going on when she got here. I told her the police were here but couldn't explain over the phone why. I got angry with the police, I would cry, I would smoke another cigarette, have another cup of tea, I just didn't know what was happening, I felt so alone once again and very frightened. I felt so intimidated in my own home and I hadn't done anything wrong.

The officer explained about Operation Ore. It was the biggest British police operation intended to prosecute thousands of users of child pornography websites, this was massive and I can't believe I was part of it. I'd know more about the operation as time went on. Child abuse is the worst thing a man could be accused of. "I'd rather be accused of murder than that" he said.

I still to this day don't believe Richard did anything on purpose, it just wasn't in him. I know we all have our little fantasies etc but looking at kids wasn't one of Richards and I'll always stand by that. I think what made things worse was the way the police dealt with the whole thing, innocent families treated like criminals, in front of children. I wish I'd of had the strength to take this all further, to have got in touch with other families that had gone through the same thing but I went through so much at the time I didn't have it in me.

The officer told me that they had also gone to Richard's house where they had explained everything to his Mum and her reactions were the same as mine. They had officers down there searching through the house for any evidence, had taken his computers and any other equipment they thought would hold any information. He told me they needed to search through my house, why? I hadn't done anything, this wasn't fair, and I didn't want some stranger looking through my belongings. He said they had to get a computer expert in to look through my internet files and to see if there was anything incriminating on there then they would have to take my pc away.

I was a quivering wreck it just felt like my whole world had come to an end. The officer said to me "We know all about you two", know what exactly?!

We were seeing each other and he looked after me because everybody else had taken the piss, we didn't live together, he had his home and I had mine.

Maria my carer turned up and it was so nice to see a familiar friendly face. I explained to her what was going on and she was shocked like me and couldn't believe it either. I didn't send Erin to school that day, I wanted her at home with me. I didn't want some copper playing with Erin, it felt like I had no control over anything anymore. She was as good as gold and sat watching the Disney Channel all day. "Mummy, why are the police here?" Erin asked and I just made something up, I can't remember what.

I think there were two female officers who started searching through my things. Different people kept turning up; everything was a bit of a blur to be honest. Before they started their search an officer had to video my house so they had proof they hadn't caused any damage to anything and they had left it like they found it. They video taped all rooms that they were searching through which was the kitchen, the living room and my bedroom. I don't think they went into Erin's bedroom, the spare room or the bathroom and by the time they got to my bedroom they'd called it a day and gave up. I had lots of Marilyn Monroe memorabilia in the bedroom and I didn't want them touching it, in the end they left it alone. They had white gloves on and went through every book, took pictures down off the walls, opened the backs and looked inside, any notes lying around they would read and if it didn't make sense they would ask me what it meant. I had a see-through bag on the shelf in the kitchen with something bought back from Althorp and they started looking through that. "That's just stuff on Princess Diana" I said all sarcastically because I just couldn't understand the depths they were going to.

The computer expert turned up, we took her to the bedroom where my pc was and she started looking through the files, we left her to it because she said it could take awhile and we went and had yet another cup of tea and another cigarette.

After a little while we went back in to see how she was getting on and she said "I'm going to have to take the hard drive with me",

No! I needed my computer for everything. I needed it for e-mail, I was a moderator on a Yahoo Reality TV Group, I also designed and sold printed labels on Ebay which was really successful, and I needed my computer! She said she'd found images and did I want to see, I thought no not really but if she hadn't shown me I probably wouldn't have believed her. She showed Maria and me one image and we just felt sick and I just broke down, but I still didn't believe Richard would look at that. She said to Maria that because of my reaction she knew that I hadn't had anything to do with it and I was perfectly innocent. I went back into the kitchen and they were searching through my cupboards. I completely lost it,

"Get the fuck out of my house!" I was shouting

"Grace, we're just doing our job" replied the officer very sternly.

They put any item they were taking into separate plastic bags that were tagged and I had to sign to say what they were taking. Apart from my computer and webcam I can't remember what else they took, nothing important. I had everything on that computer, photos of the family, all my labels, which Richard had saved; anyway, thank God, and naughty photos of us like a normal couple would. When you take them you would never expect the Midlands Police to be looking at your bits, how embarrassing. I actually deleted these pictures but they are still on the hard drive. But after seeing the image, the computer seemed dirty now anyway.

I think the Police had finished searching around 1pm and I still hadn't heard from Richard, what were they doing to him, what were they making him say, were they treating him ok or were they treating him like the sick pervert he'd been accused of being? Once the police had gone two Social Workers turned up, a large Asian guy who wasn't taking any shit and a woman. I didn't like Social Workers and I think I was more scared of them than the police. They sat down with me and explained that they were here because of Richard's arrest; he wouldn't be able to come back to this house while Erin was here. They had concerns that he may have touched Erin and was grooming her, it just kept getting worse. If anybody ever touched Erin I would kill them and they were saying it's probably been going on under my nose for ages. I still couldn't believe it; surely I would have had the feeling that something wasn't right? Erin would have been funny with him or something, and it just didn't make sense, there was no reason for me to think this.

They said that Richard would probably be bailed on the instruction that he didn't come near the house whilst Erin was here. Who the hell was going to look after me? Maria couldn't do it, all she had her own family. I couldn't get through to them that without Richard I had no care and if I seriously thought he had done anything to Erin I would never want him back here but there was something still in me that didn't believe any of this. They also told me that Erin may have to be put on the At Risk Register, at risk from who?! Erin was loved and protected probably more than most kids because of what I went through to have her and my situation, sometimes I'm too protective.

I was told that Erin would have to talk to a Social Worker and then they would know if anything had gone on and I would have to attend a meeting with Social Workers, police officers, Erin's teacher and nurse from school to discuss the whole situation and to decide whether to put her on the List or not and how long for. I was a good Mum, I wasn't one of those Mums who didn't care about her kids and turn a blind eye to anything going on just to keep her man, if anything ever went on like that he would be gone, Erin had always come first and will continue to come first, she's my baby!

Because Richard wasn't allowed near the house when Erin was here, Erin had to stay with Maria for two weeks, they were now taking my baby from me, I knew she would be fine at Maria's but this was going to kill me but what choice did I have? If it wasn't for Maria I don't know what would have happened and this is why we're still close now, we're like sisters. If Maria wasn't able to have Erin I would have had to put up with a care agency providing my care. I couldn't go back to having strangers in my house especially at a time like this. Maybe some people would see it like I should have had the Care Agency and had Erin here but I seriously didn't know what to do and it was probably best for her not being here because of the Police, I still wanted to protect her.

Richard would care for me in the day while Erin was at school and then he would be gone by 3.30pm. Maria would pick her up from school, we'd spend time together and have tea then she would go back to Maria's for the night while Richard came back to mine to look after me in the evening. I don't know how we did it but we did, we had to, we had no other choice. They also told me that they would send someone round every evening to check that Richard wasn't here when Erin was. Maria would also get visits and she had to be Police Checked. We went from being ordinary families living our normal lives to being checked up on every day, the whole thing was over the top and unnecessary.

Just when I thought things couldn't get any worse they did. My brother Ben had been taken into hospital about a week before; he'd taken a turn for the worst with his chest infections and had Pneumonia. Mum and Dad had been up to Coventry to see him the day before and he was in a pretty bad way. I even told the Social Workers that my brother was critical in hospital and I needed Richard to be around so I could get over to see him but they basically didn't give a shit.

I phoned home to tell Mum and Dad about Richard's arrest and they were in disbelief too, they liked him, he had always looked after Erin and I well and they too had no worries or concerns about him. They said that Ben was still bad and they would phone with any further news.

I didn't hear anything for awhile, I know no news is goods news but I needed to know what was going on down at the Police Station, were they going to let him go tonight or were they going to lock him up for the night or maybe forever?!

I had a phone call from the officer who had been here that morning and he said that they were releasing Richard tonight on bail. Maria could now go home with Erin now we knew Richard was coming back. He rang me from his mobile as soon as they let him go, he had no money on him so had to walk home. I didn't ask many questions, I saved them until he got home which seemed like the longest hour ever. I just sat staring out of the window smoking fag after fag (I did eventually give up smoking about 8yrs ago) waiting to see him walk past the kitchen window.

Then he appeared, thank God! He came in and just held onto me saying sorry over and over again crying. I didn't know whether to be angry or nice, I was both. This man had turned my family upside down in one day but on the other hand it was Richard and I did love him in my own little way. He just kept saying over and over again "I haven't done anything", and I believed him.

He said the police were horrible to him; they just kept trying to put words in his mouth and trying to make him confess. They said horrible sick things about our relationship; basically they were saying that Richard must be some kind of pervert with a weird fetish for being with someone disabled like me, how dare they! They came up with a story about Richard and I going on the webcam for all to see and had sex, I don't think so and have no idea where that tale had come from! I hardly went on the webcam because I'm too scared of looking fat or stupid let alone having sex in front of everyone, it just made me feel sick. They made me feel like a worthless freak that wasn't normal, I'm as normal as the next woman, just different that's all.

Richard had been bailed for three months; he had to go back to the police station on the 25th February 2003. He was just heart broken that he had caused all this upset for me and for Erin, we didn't deserve this, we'd been through enough.

I had a call from my Dad; they were on their way up to Coventry because they were told that Ben probably wouldn't last the night, he'd been in hospital for the last week with pneumonia. Ben had been ill for about a year now, chest infections and now the pneumonia. He was always the stronger one but in the end I was, I would never have thought I would outlive my Brother.

I had to get to the hospital; I couldn't believe that all of this was happening at once! Richard got me dressed and called a taxi. When we got there, Ben's carer was with him and I think Gail, Ben's other carer and her boyfriend. My Brother looked so thin; he didn't really know what was going on because of the drugs they were giving him. I said hello to him but he just looked at me, his oxygen mask was on and off and he was saying stuff that just didn't make sense, it was heartbreaking. I was absolutely shattered, my eyes were sore from crying and I was basically watching my baby brother die.

Mum and Dad turned up and then Bill, a family friend we had known for years since school. We all just sat around Ben's bed, chatting trying to involve him. His breathing started getting shallower and this grey swept over his body, it was like something took him away. He looked at me as the life went from out of his body and he was gone, he was only 30. Everybody cried and hugged each other, kissed Ben and said goodbye, I just sat numb, and I don't think I even cried because I had no more tears left that day. My Dad said do you want to kiss him and I said 'no, I can't reach', I just couldn't do it. Then Bill started covering up Ben's body with a sheet and I said "No! Don't cover him up, he won't be able to see!" And that's when I broke down.

Richard and I left the hospital. Mum and Dad stayed with Ben for a little longer and then came back to mine for a coffee before heading back home. I got in and the place just seemed really weird like it wasn't mine anymore, I just couldn't get my head round what had happened that day.

I went to bed but every time I closed my eyes I could see Ben's face, his dead eyes staring back at me and I think I was too frightened to go to sleep because I knew that when I woke up this nightmare was still going on. Richard rang the doctors and asked if a doctor could come out to give me something to help me sleep but they couldn't and told him to give me some paracetamol or something for now and a doctor would be out to see me tomorrow. This was the start of addiction to my sleeping tablets; I can't go a night's sleep without them now and things just got worse.

Chapter Fourteen

Keep it Together

I woke with the phone ringing, Richard answered it and it was the Social Worker who had come round the day before, they were on my case already. Richard told him that my brother had died the night before and to leave me alone for now and he said he would ring back later. I think I was just in a daze all day, not believing what had happened the day before. Maria had taken Erin to school and was bringing her home for a few hours later for her tea and I also had to break the news that her uncle had died.

Richard went at 3pm; that was the deal, he was here when Erin wasn't. I couldn't wait to see my baby and get a big hug from her. She came running into the living room, gave me a big kiss and I sat her down and told her that Uncle Ben had died, she was devastated; this was her first experience of someone close to her dying. She asked why the police were here and I couldn't say much to her, questions like "Why did the policemen take Richard away Mummy?" what could I say?

She put the cartoons on and for a minute it felt like things were normal again but I knew my bubble was going to burst at any moment.

At about 5 pm there was knocking at the door. It was the police, what the hell did they want now, couldn't they leave me alone to grieve? It was some high up officer, a women copper and some cocky plain clothed guy. They said they were here to get more stuff. Stuff? What stuff? There was nothing else to take; they had taken what they wanted the day before! I was sobbing my heart out telling them to leave us alone especially today; they weren't having any of it. I said to the cocky one "My Brother died last night please leave us alone" I begged them.

He asked where and what time so they could check it out, oh my God he didn't believe me, why would I make that up? I was getting angrier and angrier. The woman officer was trying to be sympathetic but if they gave a shit they would have left us alone on that day.

Mum and Dad were back in Coventry picking up Ben's death certificate so I rang them to see where abouts they were and told them what the Police Officers had been saying. My Mum was fuming! "Put him on!" she said meaning the cocky one.

She told him she had the death certificate in her hands and she was on her way. Then, in marched about six or seven coppers, there was only Maria, Erin and me there, we weren't some big drug dealing killers, we weren't going to pull our guns out and take these coppers hostage, it was over the top again. Erin was here and was witnessing the whole thing, all this about protecting her, it was disgusting how they behaved.

They wanted Richard's webcam, they could have it, I didn't care, and I just wanted them out of my house! They started going through the end cupboard where all the Christmas presents were "No, not the Christmas presents, please don't!" I said and they ignored me.

I just sat waiting for my Mum and Dad with that death certificate and then they might actually leave us alone. They arrived, thank God. The other officer was sitting at the table with his paper work and in came Mum and shoved the certificate under his nose. "There you go, satisfied now? We lost our son, Grace her brother last night so now PLEASE LEAVE OUR FAMILY ALONE!" She shouted.

I really can't remember what happened next, but I completely lost it, I had the officer pinned up against my washing machine with my foot plates and I was screaming at him,

"GET OUT!",

"GET OUT OF MY HOUSE!"

Mum had to pull me back and just hold me whilst I balled my eyes out shaking like a leaf, I think if I was physically able I would have knocked the officer out. He told all the officers to stop what they were doing and to leave us alone now, finally they got the message. Mum couldn't believe the amount of coppers that were there, apparently there was a riot van down the road that they all climbed back into.

We were all so angry. Maria left with Erin when the police were here and now Richard was back, we just couldn't get our heads round what had happened. Mum and Dad were staying the night and going back home tomorrow, they had funeral arrangements to make and other things to clear up. We had something to eat from the chip shop: but I couldn't eat; a couple of chips and that was it.

My doctor had been out to see me earlier in the day and she prescribed me some sleeping tablets. To this day I'm still taking them, I find it hard switching my brain off when I'm in bed and they've helped me to sleep, some nights I'm awake all night and I say 'oh I must have had a dud one', but most nights they help me a lot. I had my first tablet that night and the buzz was great, for that last half an hour before I went to bed I didn't give a shit about anything.

That was really it for now. Richard was here in the day whilst Erin was at school, he would go at 3pm, and Erin would come home and have tea and stay until about 6pm. The protection people would come and check on us every night normally when Erin was eating her tea or watching TV. They would come in and ask Erin what she had done at school today, obviously coming in to see if Richard was here. That carried on for two weeks and it was killing me not having Erin here but I had no choice.

I had to have someone caring for me other than Maria and Richard, I needed to have Erin back home so Gail, Ben's carer, was now without a job and I needed someone so having her work for me was the ideal solution. She was a nice enough girl, young, quiet but very sweet and it just seemed the right thing to do.

* * *

We had Ben's Funeral two weeks later. I went to see him at the chapel of rest the day before. He looked peaceful, dressed in his Depeche Mode t-shirt, black jeans and shirt, his other carer had to go and buy him some boxers because he didn't have any, he couldn't be without pants could he? I wanted him propped up a little more in his coffin but they said they didn't want to disturb him, he had bent legs and his bent back so they would have laid him out as best as they could. We walked through town after seeing Ben, everyone was doing their Christmas shopping, and life was going on.

The Funeral went well, lots of people there, it's sad to think nobody gives a shit about you until your dead, well that's what it seems like. People turn up that you haven't seen for years, why didn't they do or care more when Ben was alive? I should have gone round more than I did, but I used to get angry with the doctors and it was upsetting seeing him go downhill. I think I would of gone round more if I had had my car then because it was either walking up which took about half an hour, it was ok in the summer but I can't go far in my chair in the winter, I get too cold and my muscles seize up even more, or it was getting a cab.

Although Ben had only a short life he lived it to the full when he was able. He didn't carry on with the T-shirt business for long; I think something to do with the lack of funding. He loved music as I do and played keyboard in a band him and his mates put together called '9th Wave', not my cup of tea but I appreciated what they did. They even got to do a few gigs in Coventry that was Ben's passion in the end, music. He lived independently as I have and finally got his own bungalow and had reliable carers till the day he died. He had various girlfriends; he was always popular with the girls. He met a girl online from America who came over to stay with him a couple of times, lovely girl she was and they really suited each other. She finished it with him and I think she was the one who broke his heart as he seemed to go down hill from there. As I said before I never thought I would outlive him and I know he's watching over me.

He had Depeche Mode's 'Enjoy the Silence' going into the chapel and at the end Monty Pythons 'Always Look on the Bright Side of Life', typical Ben and that got a few laughs. I've always said I wanted a big disco song at the end of mine, I want people to smile and think 'yep, typical Grace', that's our sense of humour.

Richard was at the funeral, he could be there as long as he didn't have any contact with Erin which was ridiculous, Erin couldn't understand why she couldn't speak to Richard, he'd been like a Dad to her for three years and she missed him. But I didn't go out of my way to stop the contact, we had the wake back at mine so how on earth could they be separated, everybody ignored the rule.

Once Ben's funeral was over I had to attend a meeting with the Social Workers, Erin's teacher, the school nurse and the police, the cocky officer was there who I hated. It was to decide whether Erin should be put on the 'at Risk Register' or not. John, Anne, and Maria were there with me for moral support and Richard had to be there too. I was dreading this, I'd been on the phone to Bill all week getting some advice, he'd been a social worker so knew how the system worked, I'd written pages of notes and I went into that meeting determined to be strong, they weren't going to break me!

Before we went into the meeting, somebody said something about a film on the computer of Barbie dolls having sex and that was wrong and I just thought hang on, silly videos like that are sent on your e-mail, they're only a joke so why does that make you a paedophile? It seemed like the police were just clutching at straws. The police went through their evidence and anything they had on Richard, my circumstances, Erin etc and it was very intimidating, but if I had something to say I would say it. I asked the cocky officer that if they were that bothered about protecting Erin why couldn't they come round that Tuesday when Erin was at school or later on when she was at Maria's instead of her witnessing them invading her home and seeing me so upset, they had no answer for me. They couldn't understand why I would want Richard looking after me still and John said to them that it was hard for me to trust anybody, even his own son hadn't treated me right, John always stood up for me when it mattered. All the official people thought Erin was in danger and wanted her on the Register; the only person who didn't think Erin was at risk was her teacher, the person that saw her every day. Half way through the meeting I had to go out of the room for a breather, I was getting too angry listening to them talk about us like that.

So they decided that Erin had to go on the Register for 3 months, no contact with Richard and I had to have a Social Worker come round and teach me about Grooming etc and someone would still be popping round every evening to check we were playing by their rules. I asked about Christmas and they said Richard wasn't to come anywhere near and I said so all of you will be tucking into your turkey with your families whilst mines been torn apart, cheers!

We carried on living by their rules, someone popped in most nights and Christmas was looming. My Mum and Dad had always come up and this year wasn't going to be any different except I wasn't going to follow their rule, stuff them, this family was missing Ben I wasn't not going to have Richard there either. So the plan was, Richard would come on Christmas Eve afternoon and if anybody knocked the door we would ignore it until Mum and Dad turned up. If it was the guys from the social then Richard would hide out in the garden until they're inspection was over.

That morning I had a phone call from the Indian Social Worker asking me where Richard was and I said that he was in town so he rang Richard's mobile to see if I was telling the truth, even on Christmas Eve they couldn't leave us alone, I was fuming! I rang my Dad and told him and he made a call to the Social Worker basically saying to leave me alone, "Just because your lot don't celebrate Christmas" he said to the Social Worker. He meant Indians, straight to the point my Dad.

We tried to celebrate Christmas like a normal family but it was hard without Ben there, although we did have the box with his ashes in sat on the shelf with a can of beer, that's what he would have wanted.

New Year came and went; I couldn't be bothered to celebrate anything. February was nearing, Richards bail would be up and then we would know if they were pressing charges or not. We tried to carry on as normal as possible but you could never get the thought of February out of your head, I felt sick with worry all the time.

* * *

The last time I saw Richard alive was just before he was picked up for his driving lesson. He would always be picked up from mine and then be dropped off at his Mums. He was doing really well, he had already passed his theory and we thought he'd be driving in no time. I would get a Mobility Car and life would be so much easier, we had planned this before anything happened and bless him he still kept up with his driving lessons even though money was tight.

That afternoon I'd had a letter from the social workers about Erin staying on the 'at risk' register for even longer and it read that I was a bad mother. I got really upset about it and Richard knew it had really got to me, I cried all afternoon, I wasn't a bad Mum!

He kissed me goodbye, told me he loved me; I told him to text me later and off he went. We always put the Lottery on every Wednesday and Saturday and later as Richard always had the tickets I sent him a text to find out if we'd won anything and he text back 'no luck xxx'

We always said goodnight to one another and so before I went to bed I phoned him, no answer, I text and no reply. I rang a few times and still he wasn't picking up, hmmmm maybe he was asleep already. At about 11pm his Mum rang me asking me if Richard was at mine, I told her no and that I hadn't seen him since this afternoon. She said she had sent him to post a letter at about 10pm and he hadn't come home. I was starting to worry now; this really wasn't like him, I knew he liked to walk but it was cold and where would he go at this time of night? Maria was with me and we kept trying Richard's phone every half an hour. She even slept with me because I really didn't want to be on my own and every time we woke in the night we'd phone again, but it would just ring and ring until it just kept going to answer phone. Something was definitely wrong; I had visions of him lying somewhere hurt. He'd been having abuse shouted at him by his neighbour, the neighbour had obviously seen the police carry stuff out of the house and put two and two together. I thought maybe the neighbour had got to him or something.

We woke up and the ground was covered with snow; normally I'd be excited by some snow as it looked so pretty but not this time, I felt sick with worry, what the hell has happened to Richard? Maria took Erin to school and then got me up when she got back, Richard would be due here at 9am, everything would be ok then, and he would walk past the kitchen window look in and smile like usual. But something inside of me was telling me he was never going to walk past my kitchen window again.

I spoke to his Mum and there was still no sign of him. Maria stayed with me until Gail turned up to take over. I told her what was going on and her boyfriend and his mate came round to see me, we decided that it was time to notify the police that he was missing. An hour or so later they came back; they were accompanied by a police car. Funnily enough it was the police woman who had searched my house, the one I swore at, what the hell did she want now? They came in and they said that they had some bad news; Richard had hung himself in the woods between here and his Mums. Two men walking their dogs discovered his body that morning. No, Richard would never take his own life and what about me, he loved me, he would never leave me. Did someone make him do it, did someone else do it? I just couldn't get into my head that he would do that. I would never see him again; a part of me died that day.

The officer asked if I could go down and identify him because his mum was too old, oh God I didn't know if I could or not. "Does he look ok?" I asked and she said yes and that there was nothing to worry about and I agreed to go down to the hospital with them. I had to get a taxi with Gail. Her boyfriend and mate went in their car, the police also followed. The last time I was at the hospital was the night Ben died, I felt sick, what was I going to see, I didn't want to see Richard's dead body, how much more could I handle!

A nurse led us through a door and the silence was deafening, there was a little waiting area with flowers and I was so scared. The nurse asked me to follow her and she led me to a small room, from the door way I could see it was Richard. He was on a trolley in the middle of the room with a green blanket pulled right up to his neck.

"Yes, that's him". I said.

I went into the room and sat with him, his eyes were open a little bit and I cried and cried. He didn't look too bad, a little bit pale but nothing I couldn't handle, I even asked the nurse if I could see under the green blanket and she said she would find out. She came back and said that it wasn't a good idea, he probably hadn't been cleaned up yet and sorted out, but now I'm glad I didn't see anything I didn't need to see. When I was up on the computer some nights, he would lay behind me on the bed with his hands over his chest and I used to say to him "Don't lay like that Richard you look dead" and he looked just like that.

I stayed with him for about 45 minutes, I was just willing him to wake up, at one point a noise came out from his body and I shit myself, I guess his body was still shutting down. I had to leave him, I couldn't stay there all night and plus the police officer needed to come back home with me and write up a statement. I said goodbye to him, told him I loved him and told him to sleep well.

It's amazing how lonely and scared you feel, what was I going to do now? Richard and I had been with each other every day, the only positive thing was that he hadn't been around as much the last couple of months so I was used to him not being there.

Days were quite dark, I missed him so much. It was the little things like his bread making, doing my roots for me, getting my boots on me without hurting my feet; he never walked passed the kitchen window anymore while I was sat at the table. All sorts of thoughts go through your head, why did he do it? Did someone make him do it? How could he leave me?

I learnt more over time. Social Services phoned me and told me they were dropping everything and Erin was off the Register. The Police left me alone too, now there was no Richard there wasn't a case. There would be an Inquest that I would have to attend, I would have to get up on the stand and tell the court what I knew. Richard definitely took his own life; no one else had anything to do with it. He hung himself with a wire and had climbed the tree as there was bark on his gloves, the snow had fell that night and so there were no foot prints made around his body.

I had to sort through Richard's belongings that were here and send some things down to his Mum who wasn't being very helpful and turned quite nasty but I'll come to her in a minute.

I found letters and bank statements Richard hid away in a plastic bag on the wardrobe in the spare room so I had a look through. He was in debt up to his eyeballs, loans and bank overdrafts. Letter after letter wanting their money, he owed thousands! Before the Police thing he was probably doing ok paying them off but his pay had to go down because he couldn't look after me as much and it probably all caught up with him, I had no idea. So with his debt problems and arrest he just couldn't cope, he obviously saw no way out, no light at the end of the tunnel. I've since seen psychics and every single one of them have picked up Richard. Apparently, he's always around me looking after me, he says I was too good for him and he's so sorry for what he did. He's happy now, wherever he is and I know he's watching over me. At the beginning of our relationship, my Husband seen a ghost of a tall thin man by our bed, I didn't see it but I know it was Richard with his approval.

Operation Ore ruined so many families and it took so many lives. I don't think the police really knew what they were up against and went into every home all guns blazing. There were over 7000 suspects, over 4000 homes searched, 3,744 arrests, 1,148 people charged, 140 children removed from dangerous situations at home and a staggering 39 suicides. Hard to believe we were one of those statistics and Richard was one of the 39 men that took their lives. Whilst Operation Ore did identify and prosecute many sex offenders it did result in a lot of false arrests through errors of their investigation. Innocent families were torn apart and at the time I wanted to contact other families that were going through the same thing but I really didn't have the strength. My Mum wrote a letter to the police about how our family was treated when we were in mourning for Ben; I think she got a written apology. Would I ever get an apology for the way my family was treated? I'm still holding my breath. The police have admitted now that they did get it wrong. To this day I still don't think Richard did it and his death was more to do with his debt problem but I will never know. It's sad to think so many innocent men took their lives when it could have been prevented.

Richard's funeral was on Valentine's Day. I went to see him in the chapel of rest and he looked fine, just looked asleep. He was dressed in his suit and black top and had a scarf covering his neck because his top was a v neck and would have showed the wound. He had a photo of me and him and I also put a cigarette in his pocket.

The funeral went well; Richard's Mum had fallen out with us by this time. Basically I had saved a thousand pounds which Richard had put in an account for me so I wanted it back. She argued that it wasn't my money and turned really nasty, I wasn't the lovely 'daughter in law' now, I was probably the bitch that took her son away. I was fuming, I gave Richard a life, he was the happiest he'd ever been when he was with me and the way things ended with Richard was nothing to do with me! His Mum and I wrote a couple of letters to one another, most of her letters you couldn't read because her hand writing was so bad. I was never nasty, always polite and I simply wanted my money, I was saving it for a rainy day and this day had come. Then one morning I received a letter from Age Concern telling me basically to back off and leave her alone alone, what a cheek, that woman was unbelievable! So my Dad phoned them, good old Dad again, and explained the situation and they understood and that was the last of it, I never did get my £1000 back. I was so angry with her that when the funeral directors said she wanted me to have a third of Richard's ashes but I would have to pay for the urn I told them they could stick it, I didn't agree with him being split into three and I certainly wasn't paying for them.

The Inquest went okay. I had to swear on the Bible and tell the court about his last day and the last time I had heard from him. The police said they would have actually convicted him but with the police getting it so wrong I still don't know if he was innocent or not, I guess I will never know. When it was over I was sitting outside the court and a man came up to me "I'm so sorry" he said.

It was one of the two men that had found Richard as they walked their dogs; he was there to give his evidence too. I thanked him and I asked how he looked, I guess I was just curious. And he said he was fine, his coat was all buttoned up.

When I was researching Operation Ore for this book I found an article written by a man who had been arrested for the same thing. His whole life was torn apart like ours and his wife stood by him. He was innocent and fought for his innocence, he was strong unlike Richard. He wanted to publicise Operation Ore as it had taken so many lives. I contacted him and I was shocked at how much information he gave me. I explained that we had gone through exactly the same thing and he was very understanding and helpful. He had a list of people who had been wrongfully arrested; all he needed was a name and an address so I gave him Richard's information.

I was blown away by the information he came back with. There was a single entry in the Landslide database in May 1999 in Richard's name, Richard and I weren't even seeing each other then. The website linked an entry operated by a Russian webmaster living in Kazakhstan; the webmaster ran 5 websites linked to this database with substantial fraudulent activity. Somebody, then in Australia used Richard's credit card details to sign up to a child porn website. This guy told me the credit card number, the date and time, how much the payment was and he even told me Richards password, it was all there. The IP address was definatly from a computer in Australia, not here in the UK.

In this guys e-mail he said and I quote "Finally, and this might sound trite, so I apologise in advance –don't blame him for what he did. I experienced the exact same mental torture at the hands of the police. However, I had the advantage of being ex-military. Believe it or not, I was trained in how to survive and cope with this type of interrogation".

I felt relieved and angry, at the end of the day an innocent man took his life and I have never had an apology from the police. I was just left to deal with it as if Richard's life meant nothing but at least I know the truth now.

So once again I was putting a situation behind me and moving on. Thank God for Erin, she really does keep me strong and always will but it's amazing how strong I actually am and I will always come out on the good side of anything life throws at me.

CHAPTER FIFTEEN

Till Death Us Do Part

The last 10 years have been very quiet compared to the 10 before thankfully because I don't think I could have coped with much more drama. I've only had the problems I've already spoken about earlier with carers and ex boyfriends. I saw a guy for a couple of years but he really isn't worth me writing about, I never speak about him.

The only main upset we had was my Mum being diagnosed with Breast Cancer in 2010, hadn't our family been through enough? That woman is so brave and strong. She mentioned that they might have found a lump from a routine Mammogram. You don't really take it in; the lump could be nothing until they do more tests. It was when she told me on the phone that it was cancerous and she needed to start treatment that was when it was real and I got upset. "It's ok, I don't feel ill and I'll fight it" she said.

My Nan (Mums mum) died from Cancer when I was 19, she was riddled with it. My Nan was a heavy smoker and it started in her lungs and spread everywhere.

Mum had to have about a year off work and start treatment. First of all she had to have a lumpectomy to remove the malignant tumour and then had twenty-eight lymph nodes removed from her left side. She then had chemotherapy, six lots four weeks apart from each other. After the chemo she had twenty lots of radiotherapy, every week day for four weeks. I felt really useless as I couldn't be with her whilst she was having her chemotherapy; living an hour away it wasn't easy. That's what daughters did and I felt really shit about that, Mum knows I would have been there if it was easier. My Step-Dad and even my Dad was there with her, my Step-Dad was brilliant, really looked after her.

Luckily the cancer hadn't spread so she didn't have to have a mastectomy. She did lose her hair though which was upsetting. We had a Psychic round and he picked up that Mum had cancer and that she was having chemo and so did some Reiki on her. The next day her hair started falling out so she got her Husbands clippers and shaved it all off. She sent me a photo of her hair on the floor and said "all gone".

Mum wore a scarf around her head most of the time as it was comfier but she did have a couple of wigs. One was 'The Queen', another 'Mary' and I'm sure she had a third. One of them was free from the NHS and the other she brought off e-bay. At first I didn't want to see her bald head, it was too upsetting for me. Christmas that year was hard, we had two baldies here. Anne, Erin's Nana had been diagnosed with cancer in the September and was having chemo too. We had an unveiling of two bald heads in the kitchen, Anne taking off her woolly hat and my mum whipping off her scarf, you have got to laugh.

That was a really difficult Christmas, there was Mum ill and doing food as she always has even though she was tired and Anne. Anne had been in a Hospice for two weeks and didn't have long to live and we all knew this would be her last one. We had her with us for Christmas so she was with Erin and I don't care what any of her family think of me. She had been like family for twenty years; I always saw her as my mother in law and she was Erin's Nana. Mum and Anne found a connection that Christmas I think as they were going through the same, although Anne's was terminal.

We got through Christmas. Anne passed away in the February, two days before her 60th Birthday. My Mum beat the Cancer and made a slow recovery. She was ever so poorly after her chemo sessions but I didn't see that side of it, she said it wasn't the Cancer it was the chemo that made you feel so sick. The radiotherapy wasn't as bad as the chemo, it just made her breast a bit sore and tender but at least she was done with the chemo. Once the radiotherapy was done she had 18 doses of Herceptin to make sure the cancer didn't return.

Now, 4 years later my Mum's ok, she was one of the lucky ones. She has regular check ups twice a year and takes a drug called Letrozole which is supposed to stop it returning. Fingers and everything else crossed that it doesn't come back. It is scary; I can't check my breasts like other women. I got the doctor to check me when Mum was first diagnosed, I really should have it done regularly. As for a Mammogram I have no idea how they're going to be able to do that, I can't even get close enough to the machine when I'm having my eyes checked let alone squashing my boobs!

Mum came back to work after a full recovery but was getting tired more, I think she wanted to go for as long as she was physically able but as strong as she is, even she needed to rest. Mum and her Husband took Erin to the Dominican Republic once mum was over all her treatment. Her hair started growing back and she looked so well, so healthy. She retired in January 2013 knowing that I was happy and content now and starting the next chapter of my life.

* * *

I had fallen in love twice since Richard. The first man was love at first sight, an instant attraction and the other a love that has been there for over thirty years. Mark was a mate of Tom's, they had been in the pub all day and they asked me to join them later. They weren't there when we got there but said they would definitely be back so we had something to eat. In walked Tom and this guy with him, tall, slim and dark. Mark came and sat down at our table and it was instant banter between us. I had just read a Flirting book so knew all the signs, the flirting was amazing. I was in awe of him, he just made me laugh so much and that is the most important thing. We had a great night, he came back to mine and we sat up talking all night. He said to me

"I like you….you and I are going to have a lot of fun" and we did for the next three years.

I was besotted with him. We would meet up a few weekends a month and drink, the thing is, I don't think we ever spent any time together when he was sober. Most of the time we'd sit in the local and then he would come back to mine and carry on drinking until the morning, I never wanted our nights to end. We would chat and laugh all night, sometimes he would just grab me and kiss me or he would stay the night.

When he phoned me I was so excited, just to hear his voice. He used to tell me he loved me and my heart used to melt. He would say such nice things to me like "You don't know how sexy you are, it's your hair and eyes" he really boosted my confidence.

Everybody knew we were seeing each other but we weren't and never were official and plus he was still seeing other women, I wasn't the only one. We had discussed being together and he had thought about it. There was no question that there were feelings there but Mark would never be able to give me what I wanted and commit to me. One night he turned up and he stayed the night, he held me all night and kept telling me he loved me and let's not mess around anymore, but he was gone in the morning and it was just pissed up words yet again. He liked his single life and drink too much. We would argue like a couple too, we would always apologise and sort things out. I could never get enough of him, if I knew he was at a pub I would try my hardest to be there.

Things did fizzle out though. He used to live in Bristol before he settled back in Coventry and ended up going back to Bristol to live. He didn't even say he was going, just up and left. We spoke on the phone a few times and I used to cry and say "You left me!"

I noticed on Facebook he was in a relationship with some girl down there and that was that. I have never spoken to him since. It took me ages to get over him and I'm so glad he moved away otherwise I don't think I would of ever have moved on, but that, once again is in the past.

So my last and final love and the love of my life, my soul mate was only the boy I first had a crush on when I was eleven years old, the boy from school. James and I had been all through school together and college. As I said before James and I were girlfriend/boyfriend for a couple of months when we were 13. I had always fancied him and when he asked me out in Maths I was so happy.

He left school and went to college in Coventry a year before me. There had never been anything between us apart from the kiss we had on my last night at school. We passed each other in the corridor at college but there was no flirting or anything, he was with someone. He says now that he fancied me and got quite protective when I was hanging around with Tom and the outsiders, he didn't like them and didn't want me hurt.

He left college and moved up to Great Yarmouth with his first wife and I never heard anything from him until we found each other on Friends Reunited. He was now married for the second time and had a son. He was working, played in a band, had a new wife, four step kids and a son of his own and had grown into a good looking bloke. I had an instant attraction to him once again and seeing him with his new family I was a little bit gutted.

We messaged each other and he spoke about having a college reunion here in Coventry, it had been eighteen years since we'd seen each other. He phoned me from work one afternoon; he said it was better if he rang from work as his wife would get a bit jealous. We chatted and it was so nice hearing his voice again. I helped organise the reunion as I lived in Coventry and could go and check out some places for us to meet up.

Well I didn't think that reunion would change the rest of my life, it's weird how things turn out. About forty of us met at a hotel here in Coventry, most of us staying the night there too. I needed to look good, I wanted him to think 'wow, she grew up and looks hot' and plus I hadn't seen people for years. I even got my teeth properly bleached for the occasion. I got out of the car and James was at the top of the steps grinning at me, he was on his own, his wife didn't come along. He describes seeing me as a 'Danny and Sandy' moment in Grease because I looked so good, he makes me laugh.

There was an instant attraction, God I fancied him and the banter we had was amazing. He was by my side nearly all night and there was a lot of flirting but he was married at the end of the day. I would catch James staring at me and it just made me feel great. We had such a good night, we stayed up drinking and chatting until about 3am and plus the clocks were going back so we had the extra hour. There was a funny incident with 'The Swingers'. When I've had a drink I'll chat to anyone and there was a woman who was staying there with her husband who had already gone up to their room. She was basically saying they wanted some fun with another couple so I pretended that James and I were married just to wind her up but she was serious and told me I looked like I was up for it. In the end James had to say, we're not like that, not that we weren't actually married just not swingers. It was really funny; apparently in the morning when she came down with her husband she looked really embarrassed.

At the end of the night I saw James up to his room, nothing happened, if he wasn't married something would have happened that night, I'm certain of it. I really didn't want the weekend to end; I had such a good time, caught up with people and had a bloody good laugh! Mr C from school was there with his new wife who I got on well with and we've been close ever since. It's just such a shame that we live all over the country and can't get together more.

James and I were the same the next morning, even Maria said to me "that lad keeps staring at you". There was definitely something between us and I kept thinking about him but kept telling myself 'stop, he's married!'

James and I spoke online and we were already talking about the next reunion, I was all for it as I would get to see him again. The next reunion was the following year, the college itself got involved this time. Most of the ex-students going stayed at the college over night and Mr C and his wife stayed with me. I was hoping James's wife didn't come along this time either, that would be just my luck and would have felt so uncomfortable. I think our genuine flirting would have been noted by the mrs which wouldn't have been good. James was already at the college when we turned up, had been there all afternoon. As soon as he saw me he came running over and gave me a kiss and a hug, there was definitely something between us and everyone could see that.

The college had changed so much since we were there, very institutionalised. It was more like a hospital which was quite sad to see.

We had another great night, the college now had a bar and the drinks were so cheap, a glass of wine a £1.00. I even got a game of Truth or Dare going; I was dared to ask the care staff where I could charge my Love Eggs up, and of course I asked them, I have no actual Love Eggs to charge!

James had paid for a room at the college for the night but wanted to come back with us, it was a warm evening and so we sat in the garden until about 4 in the morning. James was by my side again and had his arm around me, stroking my neck, it was lovely. When we eventually got to bed he cuddled up behind me but nothing happened again, we just held hands. I knew he was having problems in his marriage and I think he just wanted some comfort and loving.

The following day I couldn't stop thinking about him. He messaged me as soon as he got home and told me that he had a really good night. We started texting and we both admitted that we really liked each other; he said he felt like a kid again. He would phone me when he was out and about at work or if he had to drop one of the step kids over to Norwich. I knew not to text when he was at home, I would wait for him to text me first. He would message me on Facebook when he could and would always say 'good night, I love you'.

James and Mr C were best mates and when I spent time with Mr C and his wife I would quiz him all the time as he knew James better than anyone else. Mr C really wanted us to get together; he saw it as he would then be able to spend time with James too like old times. Mr C had met James's wife before and had always said they just weren't right for each other, at the reunion he said it was like we were together.

James wasn't happy in his marriage, anything between them had died long ago but James kept things together for his son James Junior. I don't really want to go into their problems, it's private but James wasn't happy. The whole family took advantage I think, he was always a taxi for them, even gave up work and became a house husband so his wife could go and do her voluntary work. I think they would have ended their marriage long before but kept things going for JJ. JJ has Aspergers Syndrome so routine is important and James leaving him at a young age wouldn't of been good. He used to say if it wasn't for JJ he would be with me.

One of his wife's kids got in at Coventry University and James had to drive him backwards and forward at term times which I thought would be handy. We arranged a weekend for Mr C and his wife to come up and stay on a weekend he had to bring his step son back to college. The plan was James would drop him and stay here the night but tell his wife he had booked a room at a Travel Lodge. The four of us had such a good laugh together and I couldn't wait to see James. Our plans were ruined though, she decided for once to go along with James, and I was so disappointed.

We did get our night together. James had tickets in London for The Stranglers but he came to stay with me instead, he pretended he was staying with Mr C and his wife in Watford. We had a nice evening, it was hard for him to relax though and he was weak too that day. He just felt guilty which was understandable, but he had got himself in this situation.

We always spoke about being together one day when JJ was older, when he would understand more but after 6 months of us being like we were he ended it. He just couldn't cope with it, he felt bad, not necessarily for his wife but bad for JJ. It did upset me, he'd write status's on Facebook about family stuff making out everything was good at home but I knew it wasn't and in the end I had to delete him because I couldn't read it anymore knowing the truth.

We had no contact for a year and half. A school reunion was coming up for its 40th Birthday and people were discussing it on the Facebook page. They were building a new bigger school so the building would soon be no more which was really sad. I wanted to see the place I spent so much time at as a kid and see some old faces and I'm glad I went. James was saying that he would like to attend, I wanted to go but it was a long way just for an afternoon. James started messaging me again, just general chat, nothing flirty, he felt bad for what happened but I just kind of said lets just leave it and move on. James said he was definitely going and so I thought sod it I'm going too.

He was already there when I got there, sat in the playground talking to a couple of our other friends. It was slightly awkward for about ten minutes and then we were fine. We walked around the school talking about our memories and chatting to old teachers. Annabel took me that day and she said everywhere I was he was and visa versa, definitely a spark between us, no doubt about that. It was his birthday that day and he had planned to go out with his wife when he got home but his wife text him and said she couldn't be bothered now and so he stayed at the school for longer. I could tell he still wasn't happy.

That was September and in December his marriage was over. The day after Boxing Day she told him that she couldn't carry on like it anymore and their eleven year marriage was over. He had a status on Facebook saying something about the only thing that mattered now was him and JJ. From that I was guessing they had split up but didn't want to come right out and ask so I spoke to Mr C's wife and she confirmed that yes, they weren't together anymore. I knew straight away that now there could be a future for us, I just had a feeling.

We started messaging properly again and he told me that he'd moved out after sleeping on the sofa for a month until his sister lent him the money for a bond and first months rent. Now he was living in a private property, five minutes away from hers and JJ went and stayed with him whenever he wanted. He phoned me for the first time on my birthday and we were on the phone for hours catching up.

I went to London for the weekend for Erin's 16th birthday meeting Mr C and his wife and I said to them that weekend. "I know I'll be the third and last Mrs Saunders".

At the time I was talking to this other guy off the internet, hadn't been talking to him for long but we had arranged to meet the week of my birthday and he let me down. He wanted to take me out again so I told James. I said basically if you want to make a go of it with me I won't meet him, I wanted him to say "Please don't meet him, I want you!"

On April 2nd 2012 it was official, we were finally an item after thirty two years, I was so happy. It was going to be hard as we lived three hours away from each other. When you're in a new relationship you want to be together all the time so it took a lot of patience, but I had been through worse.

James would come up on the Friday night and go back Sunday night, he had started work again so it was tough on him but we managed. He would have JJ one weekend and then come to me on alternative weekends unless he had a gig with his band. We would always be on the phone, we would talk before we went to sleep every night and there was Skype.

James got on with everyone, my family, my friends, it all just felt right. I loved him so much; he was my soul mate and my best friend. All those men I met desperately trying to find 'the one' and it was James all along. I think we both had to go off in our separate directions, learn things, get wiser, experience things in life, have our kids and then really appreciate each other. It's a shame we weren't together years ago but I guess the time wasn't right for us then but it is now. I would love to have had a baby with James but life didn't have that planned for us.

I was really nervous about meeting JJ, thinking what if he hates me. We'd said hello on the phone a few times but that was about it. James brought JJ up with him for a couple of days and it was fine. We had a proper family day out at Drayton Manor; he got on really well with Erin. It's quite sweet, he's the little brother she never had, well not so much little when JJ's 12 now.

James and I talked about marrying one day, there was no reason not to now, his divorce would be finalised at the end of the year. On June 3rd 2012 on the Queens Diamond Jubilee James asked me to marry him. We had a Jubilee BBQ with friends and family, Mum even had champagne flutes engraved for us with the Jubilee logo on them. I was finally engaged to the man I adored!

We were going to get married this year, 2014 but Mum and Dad suggested making the wedding sooner, made sense as we had waited thirty years anyway. I knew where I wanted to get married, I'd viewed it before and the venue was perfect. We chose a venue in Berkswell, a village just outside of Coventry that was beautiful. It's an old Tudor style hotel with a separate building for wedding ceremonies and lovely grounds. It was accessible, the ceremony room had a flight of stairs leading down to it and the function room but there was a lift. The ceremony room was like a courtyard with its trailing plants and foliage, it was the perfect place to be married. I'd looked through wedding brochures but this hotel was the only place I had viewed and fell in love with so we booked our wedding for the 23rd August 2013.

This Hotel had a Bride of the Year every Valentines Day so we were automatically entered into the competition. The first prize was £5000.00 towards the cost of your wedding and there were four other prizes such as a meal for two, a night there, dinner with a James Buble tribute and 4th prize to use the gym facilities, good job we didn't win that one! We thought the Bride of the Year would be picked by Nailcote. "You might win as they might feel sorry for you" Mum said jokingly.

It was picked out of a hat. Bride of the Year went to a couple from Solihull, The Buble tribute night went to another couple from Solihull and 3rd prize to us, couldn't believe it when they pulled out our wedding date. James and I had a lovely meal for my birthday.

James's Mum, Theresa was taken ill and admitted to hospital in the spring. She was riddled with cancer and had gone through so much in her life. She was diabetic, had IBS, had strokes and so many other things. A very strong Irish catholic lady who rubbed people up the wrong way at times, I think if we had had the time to get to know each other I think we would have either clashed or got on like a house on fire as she was feisty like me, I would like to have thought the latter. She was in a hospital in Harlow and for five weeks James was going backwards and forwards to Harlow. It was a tough time for us, I was organising our wedding and James's Mum was dying, it should have been a happy time for James but his head was somewhere else and being with his Mum was more important. I went down with him a few times, I'd met James's parents when we were at school but hadn't seen them since then, his Dad had passed away 10 years earlier.

I was nervous about meeting his Mum, I mean this was my future Mother in law, sadly she didn't live long enough to see us get married though. We had an afternoon with Mr C and his wife and then went to see Jamess Mum and it was fine, she saw me, her face lit up and she said "Beautiful'" and we sat holding her hand. James's Mum died five weeks after being admitted to hospital, she never got out of the hospital bed. She was out of pain now and reunited with her husband. The funeral was down in Colchester as that's where James's sister lived. All his aunts, were lovely and made me feel very welcome into their family.

Our wedding day was amazing. It took a lot of arranging, you don't realise what goes into a wedding but I pulled it off. I would never have done it without my amazing Mum, she paid for the venue, the wedding breakfast and our evening do. Thank you so much to my Mum who gave us the best day, we couldn't have wanted anything more only to have James's Mum and Dad with us and of course Ben. We had three candles lit during our ceremony representing the three of them, when my Dad explained to our guests why the candles were lit, it was very emotional.

I had four bridesmaids, Erin was my chief, Saj, Maria and Mrs C and I couldn't have been more proud. They looked stunning in the sage floor length chiffon dresses. The men looked so smart too, James had Mr C and JJ as his Best Men and he gave an amazing speech, thank you Mr C. James looked so handsome, I felt so lucky and JJ looked so smart and was brilliant the whole day.

Our theme was the cream gerbera flower and the colour sage. I wanted it very subtle and elegant and it all looked so beautiful. We had tall centre pieces with gerbera's and tall green leaves, sage favour boxes that had a cancer pin in each one with chocolates. We wanted something different for our favours and decided to donate to cancer as cancer had touched both our lives. Mum surprised us with a sparkly backdrop behind the top table; I was speechless when I saw the room for the first time.

My dress was the thing I was worried about. It's hard trying to find something easy to wear when most wedding gowns have bones in the front, laced up with tons of material. I originally wanted an off the shoulder figure hugging dress but this just wasn't practical. I kept searching online, I wasn't prepared to pay hundreds of pounds and plus I couldn't afford to. As soon as I saw my dress I knew that was the one. It had a heart shaped line above the boobs, the bodice had little embroidered flowers, and the skirt had two layers with the top being split at the front so you could see the layer underneath. I ordered it off eBay and it only cost me £65.00, I was a bit dubious, it looked like such a bargain but was the quality going to be any good? When the dress came I couldn't believe how gorgeous it was for the price. I had it adjusted so it fitted me properly by taking the bones out and my Mum put a split up the back as she does to all of my dresses so that I can go to the toilet. All I had to decide now was whether I wanted a veil or just flowers, I couldn't decide. I went to a Bridal shop and they helped me out, I decided on a plain ivory veil that came down to the bottom of my back and with my hair long and wavy I finally looked amazing, even if I do say so myself.

Friends from college and school came that we hadn't seen for over twenty years. Guests came from Wales, Newcastle and Hertfordshire but it's such a busy day that you just don't have time to chat long to anyone. The whole day flies by so quickly. I was so calm on the day, we had a little champagne in the hotel room before and I couldn't wait to see all our lovely guests and become Mrs Howard after all these years. The whole day went without a hitch, apart from the bride getting very drunk in the evening but hey that wouldn't have been me if I had been sober after a good party at the end of the night.

James and I were always meant to be together and now as I write this almost a year later, I'm very content. We have our arguments like any other couple but that's normal. We have virtually nothing in common which is hard sometimes. We hate each others taste in films and most music apart from the love of the 80's and programmes on TV aren't both our taste. He's very laid back and won't confront people and will always be the good guy and I will go in all guns blazing, the feisty one. James is a Virgo and I'm a Pisces and so we're total opposites but opposites attract. I know that I won't be on my own at the end of my life; James will be with me, loving me forever now. I do believe I am his rock, I know he loves and adores me and I feel so lucky to have him. I just hope I go before him, I don't think I would be able to cope if anything happened to him, it will be heartbreaking when we're eventually parted again.

We had a lovely week just outside of Bude, in Cornwall for our Honeymoon. I found a bungalow on a farm which was converted and had a wet room. This was the first proper week's holiday I'd had in about twenty years. It's a struggle to get away; it's affording it as I would have to pay for my carers too and sorting a carer out to come away for a week. I've had a few weekends away but not a whole week. How we worked my care was Saj came down with us for a few days and Jules came down the other part of the week. Jules's Dad lived about twenty minutes away from where we were staying so she spent time with him in the day to give us Honeymooners some time on our own and it worked well. At last I was married and had a full weeks proper holiday, life was brilliant.

CHAPTER SIXTEEN

Take a Bow

As I come to the end of my story I can say fairytales do happen with a lot of patience, you really don't know what's round the corner for you. And do you know what; with all the shit I've been through I bloody well deserve some happiness!

Erin is hairdressing at college after doing a year of Theatrical Make up and I'm so proud of her. Her aim is to be a Make-up artist for films, theatre or fashion shows and I can see her achieving what she wants to do as she has got an amazing talent. She won her heat in the World Skills UK competition for the West Midlands and went on to compete in the final and ranked 3rd in the whole of the UK. She's also driving now, took her four attempts but she did it and she is now whizzing all over Coventry! Erin's grown into a beautiful, funny young woman and I will be more proud in years to come. I'm just hoping that when Daniel finally comes out of prison in a few years time he doesn't cause trouble and leaves Erin to grow as she has done. I have a feeling he's going to be quite needy and over compensating, trying to make up for the lost years, he's selfish enough to be like that and I worry for her.

I do find it really hard to trust people; I think everybody is going to shit on me. I know James will never have an affair but there's always going to be that one percent doubt in the back of my mind because of how I've been treated in the past. James's really not that kind of bloke, he doesn't look at other women, well only Drew Barrymore but I don't think she's a threat!

I am getting slowly weaker, I struggle more to do things now. Some days I struggle to do my make up and dread the thought of not being able to do it myself one day, I mean can you imagine what I would look like if James had to do it! I get tired more but I have to look at it like, well I am middle aged so it's something that comes with getting older. For a middle aged SMA woman I'm doing pretty well. I'm healthy, probably healthier than a lot of people. I look younger too which is a bonus, people are always amazed at how old I am, I love it. Someone thought Erin and I were sisters once, how chuffed was I! I don't really have wrinkles and I should considering how much I used to use a sun bed. I don't know if looking young is an SMA thing as we have such soft skin, I'm certainly not complaining! I try to make an effort with my appearance. You can still look glamorous even though you're in a wheelchair. I stand out more and sometimes I get stared at, so I want to give them something nice to look at. People don't tend to stare these days not like they used to when we were little or maybe I've just got used to it now. I like to have a tan; I wear big false eyelashes and will never leave the house without make-up on. I alter clothes and shoes so I can wear them easier although you will never know as I hide things so well.

I can still feed myself; I can use a knife and fork and am able to cut my own food. If I'm having a weak day I do find it hard to lift a fork up to my mouth but I persevere, it might take me awhile but I won't ask for help. I can't manage a spoon and soup is out of the question. Rice is hard work too, I love a Fried Rice but most of it ends up in my lap! I find it hard eating if I'm not sat at a table with a fork, so eating on the go is a bit of a nightmare and that's the only time I will give in and let someone else feed me. I get really embarrassed being fed but it's either that or going without. I have to use a straw in drinks now; I used to be able to pick up a mug of tea but would never be able to do that now. I can hold the mug on my lap and then sip from the straw. I can just about lift a sandwich up to my mouth although the filling does tend to spill out, especially Egg Mayo, my favourite!

I can still write with a pen, but with the technology now how often does anybody really pick up a pen. I can type fine on a keyboard with my two fingers and refuse to use software that does it all for you, I will do it for as long I am able to. It take's me awhile to type and that's why it's taken me 5 years to write this book, but I got there in the end and I'm proud of myself.

I hate the winter. When it's cold my body struggles more. I have to wear jumpers to keep warm which weigh my arms down. I always wrap up if I'm outside because if the cold gets into my bones it's harder for me to drive my chair. In the summer I love not having to wear much and feeling free, no sleeves making my arms feel stronger. I just feel so much healthier in the summer, my skins nicer and the sun brings out the best in you.

I take various medications every day and night. In the morning I take Primrose oil to help with my PMT although I'm not too bad, a little tetchy the week before but not as bad as some women. The slightest thing can make me cry when I'm due on but it's just my hormones. I take Salbutamol which is given to Asthma users because it's been proved that it helps with muscle weakness. If I don't take it for some reason I do feel slightly weaker which is really strange. At night I'm still taking a sleeping tablet, I feel I just can't switch off some nights so it helps me to relax. I have one Diclofenac which keeps my joints relaxed. Before I started taking them it used to take me half an hour to lie down as my hip would be stiff and I'd be in so much pain when it clicked into place but now I lie down straight away with no pain. I also have to have Omeprazole due to taking the Diclofenac to prevent stomach ulcers.

I don't have one of those big all singing, all dancing electric wheelchairs that go up and down, spin round and cooks your dinner for you, I just have a normal council one. It's comfortable and I don't have the added pressure of worrying about paying for it when it needs fixing or I need new batteries. The BMW of wheelchairs can cost up to £18,000, I haven't got that kind of money so I would have to find sponsors and get in touch with various charities.

I now have a ceiling hoist in the bedroom which makes life so much easier, no more manoeuvring a hoist in a tight spot trying not to bash my feet. I just get hooked up and off I go onto the bed, so much easier! I also have a hoist which is left in the bathroom for when I need the toilet or I need to be transferred onto the shower chair. The hoist is also a mobile one which folds small enough to get it into the back of the car if I'm staying away from home.

My body is always in a sitting position I guess, I haven't been able to straighten my legs for years and now they are at a permanent right angle, if they are pulled forward it hurts me. My arms are the same although not quite so bad as my legs as I use them more. My hands have always bent outwards but they have now got worse and I tend to do every day things with my index fingers. My neck muscles aren't too bad yet, pretty strong considering they're holding this massive head up. We all have slightly over sized heads, not in proportions to our bodies, we just say it's because of all the brains we have! My breathing is fine too; I don't struggle with my breathing when speaking like some SMA sufferers do.

I still go to concerts, we were lucky enough to see Beyonce this year. Erin and I love musicals and regularly go to Birmingham to see a show. I love to shop! It's so nice now Erin's older spending quality time with her before she eventually leaves home and has her own family. I love the days when we do lunch and then go shopping. James and I love to eat out, not too often because the budget won't stretch that far but having a romantic meal and wine is my ideal evening. And now I'm getting older one bottle of wine can see me through an evening nicely, I tend not to drink a lot now as I get ill and I can't handle the hangovers. I have a Westie dog that is just the cutest dog ever and has always been so well behaved. He literally follows me round the house especially when I'm on my own, love that dog so much!

Being stubborn helps a lot I think, I have a family to keep going for and plus what would everybody do without me eh?! I'm not going anywhere yet, hopefully with the right medical advice and support there's at least another twenty five years in me! I recently attended the National Hospital for Neurology and Neurosurgery in London to get checked out. I had their care at the beginning of my life and now I'm the end of my life I wanted their care again and for them to help me live for as long as possible. I had a chat with the doctor and we spoke about my medical history and I am to go back every year now to keep an eye on me. I had a blood test and they double checked the SMA, can't believe a simple blood test can detect the gene now. He was concerned that I'd had three chest infections together the year before because of my poor respiratory system and concerned because of my brother. As long as I have antibiotics as soon as I become ill and have flu jabs every year, which I do, I should be ok.

There's a lot of awareness for babies and young children with SMA but not enough about adults. My goal is to be the oldest surviving SMA sufferer; I believe there's a guy who's 55 as I write this. I won't just have Erin and James to keep going for, hopefully I'll have grandchildren to love and spoil.

James works full time; I have my carers when I need them and Erin's at college. It's nice now to be off of benefits as James works, to be able to pay our own rent and live as a proper family. JJ comes to stay with us during school holidays and we have family days out. It's just nice being a normal family; it's the little things in life that make it everything worth while.

James has very weak days due to his MD. He can go for weeks where he feels strong and has no problems as long as he takes his medication he lives a normal life. Over night he can be weak, struggles walking and will use his wheelchair. This can last up to a week and then he's back to normal again. It's hard to see him struggle as like me he's stubborn and won't ask for help but I like to help as he helps me, just having him lean on my chair so he can stand up makes me feel useful. He gets tired quicker now but I admire him so much, he works full time and has never had a day off work with his current job even when he's having a weak day. We're a good team together, he knows my struggles and I know his and we're crazy about each other!

I never ended up going to University, running a business or helping the community in any way, I just wanted to be a Wife and a Mum like a normal woman and I succeeded. I had to go through a lot to get here but I did it! But now I've written this I'm hoping people will contact me if they need any advice. I want to be an inspiration and show children with SMA that they have a future and can achieve things in life; it doesn't stop you from doing anything. Dr's tend to just go on about life expectancy to the parents with an SMA child but I am living proof that we are living for longer these days with the right care and support we are living full and normal lives.

That's my story, I hope it's helped a few people, helped you pass a bit of time. Helped a sufferer with SMA, helped a parent with an SMA child and helped someone who has had similar dealings with the police. Please don't judge me, I've made mistakes in life but I'm just human at the end of the day and as I've said I'm no angel.

I've tried and I am living the most normal life I can possibly live. I'm in the second part of my life now and it's time to just relax and enjoy what ever life now throws at me. But please, no more drama's and if one comes along then all I can say is ....It's one of them!